EMERGENCY EMPLOYMENT

Howard W. Hallman

EMERGENCY EMPLOYMENT

A STUDY IN
FEDERALISM

THE UNIVERSITY OF ALABAMA PRESS
University, Alabama

Library of Congress Cataloging in Publication Data

Hallman, Howard W.   Emergency employment
Includes index.
1. Unemployed—United States.   2. Economic
assistance, Domestic—United States.   3. Federal
government—United States—Case studies.
I.   Title
    HD5724.H2755   331.1'377'0973   75-20323
    ISBN 0-8173-4832-8

Copyright © 1977 by

THE UNIVERSITY OF ALABAMA PRESS

MANUFACTURED IN THE UNITED STATES OF AMERICA

CONTENTS

TABLES

PREFACE

When Congress enacted the Emergency Employment Act of 1971 and President Richard M. Nixon affixed his signature, the United States had its first nationwide public-job-creation program since the 1930s. Although such a program had been advocated by liberals during the sixties, it had never got further than one Senate vote in 1967, when a proposed program lost by five votes. Congressional Democrats tried again, and in December, 1970, passed a bill, only to have it vetoed by President Nixon. Seven months later, another such bill was acceptable to the President, and he signed it in July, 1971.

Beneath these events lies a deeper story about how the national government functions when members of one political party control Congress and a member of another party is President. This is no exceptional situation because eight of the fifteen Congresses elected since the end of World War II have been controlled by a political party opposite to the President's. In 1947 Republicans took control of Congress for a term while Democrat Harry S. Truman was in the White House. Three of the four Congresses which met during the Republican presidency of Dwight D. Eisenhower were run by the Democrats, and all three Congresses faced by Republican Nixon were under Democratic control. Not long after Gerald R. Ford, a Republican, took over the presidency from Nixon, Democratic control of Congress was extended another two years. Only during Eisenhower's first two years has a Republican President had a Republican Congress to work with, but Democratic Presidents have been paired with six Democratic Congresses.

Thus, in the postwar years party division between the legislative and executive branches has occurred slightly more frequently than united control, mostly with a Republican in the White House and Democrats in charge on Capitol Hill. This makes it important to understand the dynamics of a divided government. The Emergency Employment Act provides a suitable case history for such a study.

But there is more to American government than enactment of legislation. Laws must be carried out and programs must be administered. More often than not this is a task which not only involves agencies of the national government but also requires the participation of state and local governments. This can lead to a complicated set of relationships. It encompasses relations between the Washington headquarters of national agencies and their networks of regional offices scattered across the nation. It involves national-state, national-local, and sometimes national-state-local relations. And it also gets into the intricacies of local governmental organization, which is no simple affair because in most states the municipal units and counties serve the same territories, and in some cases metropolitan and multicounty units carry out certain functions.

These complications entered into the administration of the Public Employment Program (PEP), the name adopted by the U. S. Department of Labor when it began to implement the Emergency Employment Act (EEA) in July, 1971. Thus, this program can serve as a case history of the federal sytem in operation. This book therefore considers the Emergency Employment Act as a study in federalism, taking into account both congressional-presidential relationships and the involvement of different levels of the federal system.

Information for the case study was drawn from a host of sources. The legislative history came from congressional and presidential documents and from interviews with committee staff members on Capitol Hill, with principal participants from the Executive Branch, and with lobbyists from involved interest groups. The story of organizing and operating the Office of Public Service Employment in the U. S. Department of Labor was derived from interviews with top staff and analysis of regulations, guidelines, and progress reports. Case studies written under the auspices of the National Manpower Policy Task Force provided descriptions of local programs, supplemented by special studies by such organizations as the General Accounting Office, the National League of Cities/U. S. Conference of Mayors, the National Urban Coalition, the National Civil Service League, the Center for Governmental Studies of Washington, D. C., and the Center for Labor and Manpower Studies at Temple University. Information about the two demonstration programs was drawn from reports of the National Planning Association and Auerbach Associates. Quantitative data about program results came from the Agent Information System maintained by the Labor Department and a longitudinal evaluation conducted by Westat, Inc. Studies by J. A. Reyes Associates, Inc. and American Indian Consultants were also drawn upon.

In addition to these sources, I have had the benefit of first-hand acquaintance with efforts to establish and operate public-service employment. I first became involved with manpower programs in 1962 as deputy director of Community Progress, Inc., in New Haven, Connnecticut. In 1967, as director of a poverty-program study for the Senate Subcommitee on Employment, Manpower, and Poverty, I helped draft the first "Emergency Employment Act," which failed enactment. In the course of my work with the Center for Governmental Studies, I have conducted field surveys having to do with local and state manpower organization and specifically with the "transitional" aspects of the public-employment program.

This study was supported in part by a grant from the Ford Foundation. However, neither the foundation nor the board of directors of the Center for Governmental Studies bears any responsibility for the views expressed. The responsibility is mine alone.

September, 1975   HOWARD W. HALLMAN
                                                              President
                                      Center for Governmental Studies
                                                       Washington, D.C.

EMERGENCY EMPLOYMENT

To my mother and to my father,
in memoriam

PROLOGUE

On December 16, 1970, President Richard Nixon vetoed the Employment and Manpower Act of 1970. This bill, which had been worked out by a conference committee of the Senate and the House of Representatives, contained provisions intended to consolidate a host of existing manpower programs and to create a four-year, $2-billion program of public-service employment. The President objected that some categorical manpower programs had been left unconsolidated, but he reserved his strongest language for an attack on the public-employment program:

> The Conference bill provides that as much as 44 percent of the total funding in the bill go for dead-end jobs in the public sector. Moreover, there is no requirement that these public sector jobs be linked to training or the prospect of other employment opportunities. W.P.A.-type jobs are not the answer for the men and women who have them, for government which is less efficient as a result, or for taxpayers who must foot the bill. Such a program represents a reversion to the remedies that were tried thirty-five years ago. Surely it is an inappropriate and ineffective response to the problems of the seventies.[1]

But on the following July 12, Nixon signed the Emergency Employment Act of 1971, which authorized a two-year, $2.25-billion program of public-service employment with no consolidation of manpower programs. At the bill-signing ceremony, he remarked:

1

As you know, this is the Emergency Employment Act of 1971. It meets the objections to the bill I vetoed last year. The bill is transitional, providing for 150,000 jobs over the next two years. It also provides for job training to move people from public service jobs to jobs in the private sector.[2]

Were the public-employment provisions of the two bills all that much different? Yes and no. Congress had sprinkled the new bill with the phrase "transitional employment" and had provided for a two- (rather than four-) year program so that it would be temporary. But the annual budget figure was doubled, the kinds of jobs contemplated were essentially the same, and the provisions for training were similar.

What really brought about the change? Politics. The President's "economic game plan" to combat inflation had increased unemployment during 1970, and the unemployment rate had remained high between December and June. In Republican circles there was growing unrest about this situation, and by the summer of 1971 the President was in the process of modifying his economic policies. His acceptance of public-service employment was one manifestation of this change.

Political considerations also entered into the actions of congressional Democrats. Many of them had long championed public-service employment, and at this particular time they were well aware of the political benefits Democrats might reap by pushing for more jobs in a lagging economy. Even if their bill was vetoed, the Democrats could take credit for at least trying to do something about unemployment.

But by June, Nixon recognized the need to accept some kind of job-creation program, and the Democrats were willing to make the necessary accommodations in their legislation in order to produce a bill which the President would sign. From political compromise the Emergency Employment Act emerged.

In the background of these political events were two sets of ideas about the role of government in economic affairs generally and in specific efforts to promote job opportunities. Nixon and his advisers held one set of beliefs, the Democratic leaders of Congress, another.

Yet, ideology is not polarized completely, for both sides have many opinions in common. For instance, all presidents who have served in the past twenty-five years—Truman, Eisenhower, Kennedy, and Johnson—would have agreed with a statement of Nixon's Council of Economic Advisers:

> Besides controlling general monetary and fiscal policies, Government must establish the necessary framework for economic activity if our free and open economy is to keep its responsive and effective character. . . . It must establish the "rules of the game" for private participants; it must facilitate competition and improve the efficiency of markets; it must impose detailed regulations where the market does not offer sufficient safeguards to consumers' interests because of inevitable monopolistic conditions; and it must establish rules for its own participation in market activity.[3]

But it is doubtful that his Democratic predecessors would have agreed with Nixon when he said, "personal freedom will be increased when there is more economy in government and less government in the economy."[4] The Democrats have been more inclined to believe that personal freedom requires greater economic security and that this necessitates an assertive role for the federal government, including substantial government spending. Truman, for example, asserted: "Public spending, as determined by the Congress and other legislative bodies throughout the Nation, represents a continuing determination by the people as to what part of their total productive power they wish to devote to the things which they must do together instead of doing separately."[5]

Between the Democrats and the Republicans, the dispute is, then, a matter of degree. It is not a choice between diametrically opposed economic systems, such as socialism versus capitalism, for both parties believe in a mixed economy. Rather their disagreement relates to the proper mix and to the extent of governmental intervention in the economy compared to dependence upon private market forces.

In this ideological context arose the idea of job creation through federal spending for public-service employment. The value orientation of liberal and middle-of-the-road Democrats, and some liberal Republican allies, made them sympathetic to the idea, while mainstream Republicans, joined by conservative Democrats, were inclined to oppose it. This underlying ideological difference had a strong effect on legislative efforts to adopt a public-employment program. Thus, both ideology and politics were interwoven in the events which led to enactment of the Emergency Employment Act.

PART ONE
LEGISLATIVE PHASE

1

PUBLIC-EMPLOYMENT
PROPOSALS
IN THE SIXTIES

Ever since the 1930s, when the New Deal created millions of new jobs under the Public Works Administration (PWA) and the Works Progress Administration (WPA), the idea of public-service employment has repeatedly cropped up. In the sixties it got its first major boost from the Senate Committee on Labor and Public Welfare—a natural place because it is one of the most liberal committees on Capitol Hill.

This happened in 1963, when Joseph S. Clark of Pennsylvania, at the start of his second term in the Senate, became chairman of the committee's Subcommittee on Employment and Manpower. In May, the subcommittee embarked on a study of the nation's manpower problems, and during the next ten months it held fifty-six days of public hearings. In April, 1964, the subcommittee issued its findings and recommendations, including a proposal that "Federal, State and local governments should undertake a joint program to directly employ the hard-core unemployed in poverty-stricken areas, both rural and urban."[1] In that month the national unemployment rate was 5.4 percent, down from a peak of 6.7 percent in 1961.

Much the same idea had been considered a few months earlier by President Johnson's Task Force on the War on Poverty, but it had been rejected because of the high cost. Instead, Johnson proposed the Economic Opportunity Act, which created the Job Corps, the Neighborhood Youth Corps, and the Work Experience Program for welfare recipients. The last two and certain rural operations of the Job Corps contained elements of direct employment, but all were presented basically as training programs rather than job-creation activities. Congress enacted the bill, including the soon-to-be controversial Community Action Program, with very few deviations from the version drafted by the Executive Branch. (This illustrates the way in which legislative initiative is exercised by the White House when the same party controls both branches. A different set of dynamics operates when control is divided.)

But the idea of publicly created jobs kept cropping up in reports of various presidential commissions which were appointed to study some of the complex problems confronting American society. Each commission in turn concluded that employment was part of the solution to the problem it was studying and that some form of subsidized public-employment program was necessary. These commissions, the years they reported, and their job clienteles were as follows:

> National Commission on Technology, Automation, and Economic Progress (1966), for the "hard-core unemployed"
>
> President's Commission on Law Enforcement and Administration of Justice (1967), for youth
>
> National Advisory Commission on Food and Fiber (1967), for rural areas
>
> President's National Advisory Commission on Rural Poverty (1967), for rural areas
>
> National Advisory Commission on Civil Disorders (1968), for urban ghettoes
>
> President's Commission on Income Maintenance Programs (1969), for welfare recipients

Meanwhile, Congress was nibbling at the edge of the jobs question. In 1965, Senator Gaylord Nelson of Wisconsin secured passage of an amendment to the Economic Opportunity Act designed to provide jobs for conservation and beautification activities in rural areas, a program known as the Nelson Amendment for a couple of years until the Johnson administration renamed it Operation Mainstream. In 1966, Representative James Scheuer of New York successfully sponsored an amendment to the same act which created a special New Careers program intended to provide training and new jobs for paraprofessional workers in various health and welfare agencies. These were both relatively small programs, together totalling $73 million for about 21,000 jobs in the 1967 fiscal year.

Urban civil disorder, which reached a peak in the cataclysmic Newark and Detroit riots in the summer of 1967, gave rise to the most serious legislative attempt to enact a public employment program. Though national unemployment was below 4 percent, black unemployment was twice that rate and one out of four black youths was unemployed. Believing that more jobs for ghetto residents would help to relieve one of the causes of unrest, Senator Clark and Senator Robert Kennedy of New York and their staffs drafted the "Emergency Employment Act of 1967," which called for expenditure of $2.8 billion in two years. With the support of Jacob Javits of New York, a liberal Republican and ranking minority member of the Labor and Public Welfare Committee, they attached it to the Economic Opportunity Amendments of 1967.[2] In an effort to gain more Republican support, Clark negotiated with Winston Prouty of Vermont and Minority Leader Hugh Scott of Pennsylvania to produce a compromise which reduced the authorization to $875 million until expended. This came to the Senate floor toward the end of September in the form of a Prouty amendment, which lost by five votes.[3]

The defeat can be attributed mainly to the opposition of President Johnson, who by then was deeply involved in expanding the Vietnam War and was opposed to so large an increase in the domestic budget. The White House staff was able to line up the Senate leadership against the bill and this, combined with the expected opposition of southern Democrats and conservative Republicans, was sufficient to kill the measure. From outside, notable support for emergency employment came from the AFL-CIO, the National League of Cities, the U. S. Conference of Mayors, and the newly formed National Urban Coalition. But to no avail.

On the House side, Representative James O'Hara of Michigan was then a leading force in the Select Subcommittee on Labor, the unit of the House Committee on Education and Labor with jurisdiction over manpower programs. In the fall of 1967, O'Hara introduced a "Guaranteed Employment Act" in the House of Representatives. A few months later Representative John Conyers of Michigan proposed a "Full Employment Opportunity Act" as one of several measures intended to give legislative form to a "Freedom Budget" drawn up by civil-rights organizations. But these bills never emerged from committee. Senator Clark introduced a revised bill in 1968, but this also died in committee. The National Urban Coalition and the U. S. Conference of Mayors conducted a survey demonstrating that plenty of useful jobs could be created, but the real obstacle was fiscal limitations in a war-swollen budget.[4]

The liberal Democrats, with some liberal-Republican support, pressed for public-service employment because they saw that even when the national unemployment rate fell below 4 percent, as it did in 1966, the black unemployment rate was twice that of whites and teenage unemployment was four times the national average. In the liberals' view, full employment would not be achieved until the rates for these population groups were substantially reduced. But southern Democrats, conservative Republicans, and President Johnson all continued to oppose new federal expenditures for this purpose, and Congressional liberals were no match for this opposition. Eight years of Democratic control of the Executive Branch ended with a beleaguered group of liberals in Congress still talking about a public-employment program but having no legislative success.

2

LEGISLATIVE ACTION
IN 1969 AND 1970

Not unemployment but inflation was Richard Nixon's major economic concern when he became President on January 20, 1969. At the time, the national unemployment rate was 3.3 percent. the lowest rate since 1953 (during the Korean War), but prices had risen nearly 4 percent in 1968, compared to an average rate of 1.5 percent per year during the early sixties. At a news conference a week after his inauguration, the new President stated his conviction that

> the primary responsibility for controlling inflation rests with the national administration and its handling of fiscal and monetary affairs. This is why we will have some new approaches in this area. We assume that responsibility. We think we can meet it, that we can control inflation without an increase in unemployment.[1]

In March he sent Congress a special message on fiscal policy in which he stated: "Only a combined policy of strong budget surplus and monetary restraint can now be effective in cooling inflation."[2] He was counting on the Federal Reserve Board to exercise monetary restraint, and on the fiscal side he proposed in April that Congress cut $4 billion out of the federal budget which outgoing President Johnson had submitted in January.

Nixon worked out his economic policies with a group of advisers known as the Troika: Paul W. McCracken, chairman of the Council of Economic Advisers; David M. Kennedy, secretary of the treasury; and Robert P. Mayo, budget director. He also had the advice of Arthur F. Burns, a counselor to the president in the White House Office, formerly chairman of the Council of Economic Advisers when Eisenhower was president and in the interim a professor of economics at Columbia University. Before their appointments, Kennedy and Mayo had been officers of the same bank in Chicago, and McCracken had been an economics professor at the University of Michigan. Also on the Council of Economic Advisers were Herbert Stein from the Brookings Institution and Hendrik S. Houthakker from Harvard University. (From its beginning, most CEA members have come from the academic world and have returned there following government service.)

While this set of advisers was helping the President prepare, carry out, and eventually modify the "economic game plan," another group from the administration was seeking to develop and obtain passage of legislation related to manpower programs. This was mainly the responsibility of officials at the Department of Labor: Secretary George P. Shultz, Assistant Secretary for Manpower Arnold Weber, and Deputy Assistant Secretary Malcolm Lovell. Their effort was coordinated with administration policy by the Bureau of the Budget, particularly through Assistant Director Richard Nathan. Shultz and Weber came from the Graduate School of Business of the University of Chicago; Lovell had served as a state official in Michigan under Governor George Romney; Nathan, a political scientist, came to the government from the Brookings Institution. In their approach to manpower programs, they were oriented more toward reorganization and management reform than toward program expansion, but they would need time to develop a legislative proposal.

By 1969 virtually all manpower experts in the country agreed on the need to consolidate the multiplicity of manpower programs which had sprung up during the preceding eight years. Before 1960, there were two principal networks of manpower agencies: the federal-state employment services, which handled unemployment insurance and labor-market exchange activities, and the vocational-education system, run by the states with federal grants. In 1962, Congress enacted the Manpower Development and Training Act to provide retraining for persons displaced by technological change and lagging local economies, and it divided administrative responsibilities between the employment service and the vocational-education agencies. But these were old and sluggish insitutions, slow to respond to new perceptions of problems, particularly the need to serve more youth and to reach unskilled and undereducated persons more effectively. For that reason, the manpower programs in the Economic Opportunity Act of 1964, which began President Johnson's War on Poverty, by-passed the older agencies in favor of newly organized Job Corps centers, community-action agencies, and other local organizations. In the burst of legislation of the next four years, these two basic acts—MDTA and EOA—were amended several times to set up new programs for special categories of need, and the Office of Economic Opportunity and the Department of Labor designed additional programs. By 1969 proliferation had become excessive.

That some kind of consolidation was needed was recognized on Capitol Hill. But Congress, too, would need time to gear up for manpower-reform legislation because the two subcommittees with jurisdiction had new leadership: Gaylord Nelson, who became chairman of the Senate Subcommittee on Employment, Manpower, and Poverty after Clark failed to win re-election, and Dominick Daniels of New Jersey, who took over as chairman of the House Select Subcommittee on Labor following the death of the previous chairman, Representative Elmer Holland. Daniels took the post on the basis of seniority instead of O'Hara, the House's chief manpower expert. However, they agreed that for the coming session O'Hara would continue to carry the initiative for manpower legislation, while Daniels concentrated on occupational health and safety, a legislative topic of major importance that year.

Republican William Steiger of Wisconsin, who had made manpower problems his specialty when he entered the House in 1967 at the age of twenty-eight, introduced the first manpower bill[3] in the House on May 5. O'Hara followed with his own bill[4] on May 26. Both bills called for reorganization and consolidation of federal manpower programs, and O'Hara's bill contained additional provisions for public-service employment, an activity not included in the Steiger bill.

The Nixon administration was not ready with its own proposal until August 12, when the President simultaneously announced four domestic program initiatives: manpower reform, welfare reform, general revenue sharing, and reorganization of the Office of Economic Opportunity. Soon after this he sent Congress a special manpower message containing seven specific recommendations:[5]

1. Consolidate major manpower development programs
2. Provide flexible funding
3. Decentralize administration of manpower services to states and metropolitan areas
4. Provide more equitable allowances for trainees
5. Create a career development plan for trainees
6. Establish a national computerized job bank
7. Authorize the use of comprehensive manpower-training system as an economic stabilizer.

The first six items dealt with administrative improvements in the manpower system. The seventh envisioned a 10 percent increase in funds for manpower services whenever the national unemployment rate rose above 4.5 percent for three consecutive months. The increased funds would be for services not jobs, for Nixon did not propose job creation as part of his manpower package.

Along with his message to Congress, the President sent a draft of a bill which was introduced by request in the Senate by Jacob Javits and in the House by William H. Ayres of Ohio, the ranking Republican on the Education and Labor Committee.[6] Both were joined in sponsorship by other Republicans on the two labor committees and by the minority leaders of the two houses. These bills were referred to the labor committees and then assigned to the subcommittees headed by Senator Nelson and Representative Daniels. The Daniels subcommittee also had the Steiger and O'Hara bills to consider.

The Nelson subcommittee commenced hearings on November 4, 1969, with Secretary of Labor Shultz as the first witness, and ultimately held twenty-one additional days of hearings, lasting into May, 1970, and including field hearings in six cities.[7] As the hearings progressed, subcommittee staff—William Bechtel, William Spring, and Richard Johnson—began drafting a bill, which became S. 3867 when introduced by Senator Nelson on May 20, 1970, the day before the hearings were completed. Like the O'Hara bill, the Nelson bill provided for a public-service employment program, in addition to consolidation of existing manpower legislation, thus combining Democratic and Republican interests. It also set up new categorical programs on environment improvements and Indian manpower services, a reflection of individual members' interests in special issues. A week later Senator Prouty introduced another bill[8] dealing only with consolidation of manpower services in a manner somewhat different from the administration bill.

When the committee went into executive session, it chose the Nelson bill as the one to "mark-up." This process extended through June and into July, owing to the senators' busy schedules and competing demands for their attendance at numerous committee and subcommittee meetings. Nelson and Javits (along with their staffs) were the main participants in the process, and each held the proxy votes of absent senators. After clearing the subcommittee, the bill went to the full Committee on Labor and Public Welfare, which continued the mark-up process under the chairmanship of Ralph Yarborough of Texas.

The details of manpower reform are only an incidental concern to us here (for more on the subject, see R. H. Davidson's *The Politics of Comprehensive Manpower Legislation* [Baltimore: Johns Hopkins University Press, 1972]). The major issues had to do with the respective roles of state and local government in the control of decentralized manpower programs and with how much program consolidation there would be. The Republicans favored a greater role for the states than the Democrats did (there were then thirty-two Republican governors in the fifty states), and they were also in favor of more consolidation. In contrast, the Democrats were more interested in enhancing the authority of mayors and other local officials, and they were more responsive to groups of blacks, Spanish-speaking organizations, and rural interests who wanted to maintain categorical programs directed to their needs and conducted by them. In these matters, the Democratic majority generally had its way, favoring local government and keeping a number of categorical programs. The Democrats did, however, incorporate a number of provisions suggested by Republicans, including one from Senator

Javits which took the "trigger mechanism" which the administration bill had proposed as a method for increasing manpower-service funds and converted it to a means of augmenting funds for public-service employment.

On August 20, the committee reported the bill to the Senate.[9] In the accompanying report, three Republican senators (Javits, Prouty, and Richard S. Schweiker of Pennsylvania) recorded "supplemental views" in which they supported the concept of public-service employment while differing with some of the details of the bill adopted by the committee's Democratic majority. Three other Republicans (Peter H. Dominick of Colorado, George Murphy of California, and Ralph T. Smith of Illinois) filed separate supplemental views opposing the concept of government as the employer of last resort. The Democrats exercised their command of the Senate floor and passed the bill by a vote of 68 to 6 on September 17.[10]

The Senate-passed bill then went to the House, where it was referred to the Education and Labor Committee, which still had its own manpower bills pending before the Daniels subcommittee. This subcommittee had begun hearings on December 10, 1969, and continued them off and on in Washington and in four cities around the country through May 6, 1970, for a total of twenty-seven days of hearings.[11] The subcommittee met during the Easter recess in an attempt to start work on a bill but found itself sharply divided between Democrats and Republicans—much more so than was the case with the Nelson subcommittee in the Senate. Representative O'Hara, the lead Democrat, was much more interested in public-service employment than in manpower reform. Other Democrats shared his view, particularly after the national unemployment rate began rising early in 1970, as Nixon's restrictive fiscal policies began to produce their effects. However, the administration was adamantly opposed to public-job creation, and while some House Republicans were uneasy about the impact of increased unemployment in an election year, they supported the administration's position.

Although the Democrats had the votes to get a public-service employment bill through the Education and Labor Committee, they doubted that it would pass the House without support from liberal and middle-of-the-road Republicans needed to overcome the expected opposition from a bipartisan conservative coalition, long a powerful force in the House of Representatives. Since the House Democratic leadership would not give up its commitment to public-service employment and the Republican leadership would not support it, the impasse lasted all summer.

Two events combined to change the situation. In July, George Shultz left the Labor Department to become director of the new Office of Management and Budget, taking Weber with him as his deputy, and Undersecretary James D. Hodgson was promoted to secretary of labor and Malcolm Lovell became assistant secretary for manpower. Hodgson had been in industrial relations with Lockheed Aircraft Corporation and Lovell had held similar posts in the automotive industry. The two replacements were more pragmatic than their professorial predecessors, and Lovell in particular began to search for some way to achieve a compromise. On September 17, when the Senate passed its manpower bill with a four-year price tag of $12 billion, including $4.5 billion for public-service employment, the House Democrats got some bargaining room, and the administration had something to worry about. With congressional elections only two months away and unemployment still on the increase, both the administration and the House Republicans were eager to work out a compromise.

An indication of this readiness for compromise is reflected in the recollections of participants, each of whom recalled that he initiated the move. Lovell was ready to reach an agreement, and he talked with Republican leadership of the Labor Committee and with lobbyists from the AFL-CIO, the National League of Cities/U. S. Conference of Mayors, and the National Urban Coalition who had pipelines to the Democrats. At the same time, David Rusk, a junior staff member from the Labor Department, bootlegged to the principal Democrats and Republicans on the subcommittee an unofficial version of a suggested compromise bill. O'Hara felt there were enough points-in-common between this document and the Senate bill for something to be worked out, and he was getting signals from other sources that Lovell was prepared to reach an accommodation. But the subcommittee Republicans still held back.

To force the issue, O'Hara got the subcommittee to meet on the morning of September 29 and to report out a bill which contained only public-service employment and no manpower reform. The full committee was scheduled to take up the measure the next day. That afternoon, Lovell arranged through Representative Albert Quie to meet with O'Hara in order to seek a compromise agreement. O'Hara, along with Austin P. Sullivan and Jim Harrison from the majority staff, met at dinner with Kenneth Young, a legislative representative from the AFL-CIO, J. Thomas Cochran from the National League of Cities/U. S. Conference of Mayors, and Wayne L. Horovitz from the National Urban Coalition to work out strategy. Then O'Hara, Sullivan, and Harrison went to an all-night bargaining session involving Quie and Steiger with Michael J. Bernstein from the minority staff, Lovell, William Hewitt, and Rusk from the Labor Department, and a couple of staff from OMB. By dawn a new bill was ready. By telephone, Lovell obtained OMB clearance from Assistant Director Nathan, and Secretary Hodgson wrote the committee that the administration endorsed the compromise bill.

O'Hara introduced the product of the negotiations that morning (September 30) as H. R. 19519, with cosponsorship of both Democrats and Republicans on the Labor Committee. This bill provided for substantial consolidation of manpower programs and gave local governments a stronger role (compared to that of the states) than the original administration bill had. It also included a public-service employment program, but with language enabling the secretary of labor to set objectives for moving people into unsubsidized employment within certain periods of time and allowing him to reduce funds to programs failing to meet this objective. This was the key compromise to gain Republican support for public-service employment. Total authorization for the entire package was $7.5 billion for four years, $5 billion less than the Senate's bill, and the secretary was permitted considerable discretion in allocating the funds among different programs.

Even though most members had not seen the bill, the Education and Labor Committee took it up the same day, made two minor changes, and voted to report it to the House.[12] When the bill came before the House on November 17, Democratic and Republican leaders stuck with their compromise and no serious efforts were made on the floor to change it. The crucial vote occurred on a motion to recommit the bill to committee, which lost 275 to 80, whereupon the bill passed by a voice vote.[13] Since it differed from the Senate bill, a conference committee was needed to reconcile the two. Ordinarily conferees are drawn from the committees handling the legislation, and this was the case with the manpower bill. Perkins headed the House delegation and Nelson led the Senate conferees. They would have to deal not only with the issue of public-service employment but also with a host of other issues affecting various groups having a special interest in manpower programs.

Manpower-reform legislation had long been the focus of extensive lobbying by organizations representing state and local manpower agencies. The National League of Cities/U. S. Conference of Mayors was interested not merely in job creation through public-service employment but also in getting the program under the control of cities rather than the states. At this stage, the National Governors Conference, which might have spoken on behalf of states' prerogatives, was not focusing on manpower legislation. Far more vocal were two associations of state agencies, the Interstate Conference of Employment Security Agencies (involving state employment services) and the American Vocational Association (representing state vocational-education departments). Also, the national network of Opportunities Industrialization Centers (OIC) and the regional network of Operation SER, a Spanish-American organization in the Southwest, pushed to get support for their organizations in the legislation. The pressure from these groups persisted throughout the period during which the conference committee was at work.

The Nixon administration also asserted its views, and as conference proceedings got underway, Secretary of Labor Hodgson wrote to the conferees to express the administration's support for a bill along the lines of the compromise worked out with the House. He set forth several basic concepts of manpower reform and public-service employment which he considered to be essential. Among these were (1) the need to provide for a transition from federally subsidized public-service employment to nonsubsidized public and private employment, (2) the need to keep the level of public-service employment within realistic budget constraints, and (3) the need to apportion funds in a manner leading to comprehensive programs at the state and local levels.

To the administration, the first point was the most important. The Democrats had no quarrel with the objective of moving persons into unsubsidized employment, and the Senate and House bills both included several provisions along these lines. What bothered them was the administration's insistence on a clause in the House bill that permitted the secretary of labor to reduce the share of federal funds to any program not meeting specific objectives for transition of participants out of subsidized jobs. Although this clause allowed the secretary to take into account local economic conditions which precluded other employment opportunities, the Senate Democrats were fearful that the administration, which had never wanted public-service employment in the first place, would use this power to reduce federal support to a level which would make it very difficult for localities to keep their programs going. The Senate Democrats would not yield on this point, and the House Democratic conferees agreed to strike this clause—quite willingly, for they were also dubious about allowing so much discretion to the Department of Labor. They did this even though Lovell conveyed the message from White House staff that the President might veto a bill denying the secretary of labor such authority. However, by this time President Nixon had threatened to veto bills far more often than he had actually done so, and the Democrats did not take the threat too seriously.

As for Hodgson's second concern, the conference committee settled on $9.5 billion as the total authorization for four years, a figure midway between the $12 billion in the Senate bill and the $7.5 billion which the administration had earlier agreed to in the House bill. This sum was reached by cutting $2.5 billion from the Senate's authorization for public-service employment but leaving $2 billion for this program.

On the secretary's last point, the conference committee's bill assigned a third of the funds for comprehensive manpower services, a third for public-service employment, and a third for a new occupational-upgrading program, various categorical programs, research and demonstration projects, and administration. However, the conference agreement retained provisions of both bills to permit the secretary of labor to transfer up to 25 percent from one major program to another. This meant that public-service employment was assured at least 25 percent of the funds and could receive over 40 percent if the secretary chose. It also meant that OIC, SER, and other special programs could be funded independently of local comprehensive programs.

On the whole, the bill which emerged from conference was closer to the Senate's version than to the House bill. Some of the House Republicans felt that their Democratic colleagues had deserted them by walking away from the compromise hammered out in September, but the House Democrats considered that they were honor bound to stick with that compromise only through passage by the House, and this they had done. Once in conference their natural sympathies were closer to the Senate bill, and they sided with the Democrats from the other side of the Capitol. The House Republican conferees were so dissatisfied with the results that they refused to sign the conference report, but three of the five Senate Republicans signed it (Javits, Prouty, Schweiker).[14]

By the time the conference committee had finished its business, Congress was rushing toward adjournment. Since the House had requested the conference, it would vote last on the report. The Senate took it up on the afternoon of December 9 and finished its deliberations the next morning. All in all, the debate was desultory, the only major opposition coming from a couple of southern Democrats who were concerned about excessive federal spending. The Senate adopted the report 68 to 13, with eight southern Democrats and five conservative Republicans in opposition.[15]

That afternoon, December 10, the House considered the report in a more lively debate. Chairman Perkins, assisted by Representative O'Hara, defended the conference report against charges made by four Republicans from the conference committee that the conference bill did not go far enough in decategorizing manpower programs, that there was not sufficient funding flexibility, and that the authorization for public-service employment was excessive. Representative Quie stated that the Republicans' main reason for opposition was "the fact that this conference report does not give effective tools to the secretary of labor to move people out of public service employment to nonsubsidized private and public employment." However, the House of Representatives adopted the conference report by a vote of 177 to 159, divided mostly along party lines. This was of course much closer than the earlier key 275-to-80 vote in favor of the original House bill.[16]

During the next several days, rumors circulated that Nixon intended to veto the manpower bill. Senator Nelson wrote the President urging him to sign what he, Nelson, described as a workable compromise, and Senator Javits talked to White House staff on behalf of the bill. Nelson, Javits, and Perkins held a joint press conference to promote the bill, and municipal associations, the AFL-CIO, and the Urban Coalition urged approval and got its local affiliates to do the same. The Reverend Leon Sullivan, the Philadelphia minister who founded OIC, even got into the White House, but he could find no one to make his case to.

Secretary Hodgson and Assistant Secretary Lovell favored a veto on the ground that the conference committee had refused to go along with the administration's minimum requirements, but neither of them conferred directly with the President. Nixon's principal advisor was George Shultz, who was strongly opposed to public-service employment and recommended a veto.

On December 16, not long before he lit the National Christmas Tree, President Nixon announced that he was indeed vetoing the Employment and Manpower Act. Shultz's deputy Arnold Weber had drafted the veto message. The prologue to this book quotes the passage opposing "dead-end jobs in the public sector." The President also stated that the bill "does not achieve the reforms necessary to establish a manpower program that will serve the needs of the nation or the individual job seeker." He was talking specifically about the continuation of certain categorical programs. What he wanted was the House-passed bill, which despite some reservations, he would have signed, including its provisions for public-service employment. Nixon stated:

Transitional and short-term public service employment can be a useful component of the nation's manpower policies. This administration agreed to such a program provision in the House-passed bill and, in fact, this administration has initiated a similar public service careers program under existing law. But public employment that is not linked to real jobs, or which does not try to equip the individual for changes in the labor market, is not a solution. I cannot accept a bill which so fully embraces this self-defeating concept.[17]

The President and his advisers did not think that the language of the conference bill was sufficiently strong to get program participants into unsubsidized employment and believed that only by giving the secretary of labor the power to reduce funding would there be sufficient leverage on local sponsors to achieve this objective. Moreover, they had agreed to public-service employment quite reluctantly in September, and their ideological opposition came to the fore again after the conference had weakened program consolidation.

Since the bill which went to the President carried a Senate number (S. 3867) a vote to override the veto had to occur first in the Senate. This vote was taken on December 21, and although 48 Senators favored override to 35 against, this majority was less than the two-thirds of those voting required by the Constitution.[18] The House did not vote, since it would consider an override only if the Senate vote were successful. So the final Senate vote ended this phase of the push for a public-service employment program.

3

PASSAGE OF THE EMERGENCY EMPLOYMENT ACT OF 1971

In the wake of the President's veto of manpower legislation in December, 1970, and the congressional failure to override the veto, the Democrats were discouraged and not ready to take up the struggle again immediately. But they were galvanized into action early in January, 1971, when the Bureau of Labor Statistics announced that in December unemployment had reached 6 percent, for the first time since August, 1961. (Actually it was even worse, because later recalculations led to a revised figure of 6.2 percent.) Carl Albert of Oklahoma, the newly elected Speaker of the House, decided to make employment a major issue for the Democrats, and before the month was over Representatives Perkins, O'Hara, and Daniels had each introduced an employment bill. At the other end of the Capitol, Senator Nelson introduced a bill with broad bipartisan cosponsorship. Until they reached conference committee, the two houses pursued their separate courses, with the Senate moving along a few weeks ahead of the House.

When Nelson heard about the December unemployment rate, he instructed Bechtel, Spring, and Johnson from the staff of the Subcommittee on Employment, Manpower, and Poverty to reread President Nixon's veto message and search for clues for an acceptable jobs bill. The key sentence seemed to be this one: "Transitional and short-term public service employment can be a useful component of the nation's manpower policies." To avoid the appearance of a permanent program, the new bill would have an authorization for only two years. John Scales, minority staff counsel, suggested that the bill should utilize a trigger mechanism tied to periods of high unemployment (Javits had adopted this idea from the administration's manpower-reform bill). This was done by making public-employment funds available when national unemployment was 4.5 percent or higher for three consecutive months and with more funds authorized for each rise of 0.5 percent in unemployment; the program would terminate when unemployment receded below 4.5 percent. To help persons holding these public-employment jobs get into regular employment, the bill would take all the language of the vetoed bill which required assurances of such linkages. But Nelson remained adamantly opposed to giving the secretary of labor power to reduce funding as a means of forcing local sponsors to meet specific standards for moving participants out of special public-service employment.

As Nelson and his staff neared the completion of the bill-drafting process they began to line up cosponsors. A bill is introduced in Congress by a member either on his own or on behalf of himself and other members. Cosponsors are used when several members have similar interests, and it is also a means of lining up support early in the legislative process. Sometimes cosponsors are enlisted by the principal senator talking to other senators, but sometimes his staff contacts other staff members, who check with their bosses whether they want to cosponsor. A key sponsor would be Minority Leader Hugh Scott of Pennsylvania, who had supported the compromise amendment in 1967, and once he agreed to cosponsor, several other moderate Republicans joined in. Through this process, twenty-two Democrats and ten Republicans came to be cosponsors of S. 31, the Emergency Employment Act of 1971, when it was introduced by Senator Nelson on January 25. Later, two other members added their names, so that fully a third of the Senate was behind the bill.

The bill was referred to the Committee on Labor and Public Welfare and assigned to the Nelson subcommittee. Nelson's staff then began to line up witnesses for public hearings. This is an important task because hearings are a vital part of the Congressional process. The subcommittee chairman, the ranking minority member, and other participating members (or their staffs) absorb a lot of knowledge at hearings. (Many senators and representatives rely heavily on aural sources of knowledge—not only hearings but also briefings by their staffs, conversations with other members, committee discussion, conversations with administration officials and lobbyists, and occasionally floor debate.) Hearings also provide a forum for questioning representatives from the Executive Branch, and they are used to build a record in support of various viewpoints. The subcommittee chairman controls the witness list and order of appearance, but other members, including the minority, have the right to request the calling of specific persons. Senators and representatives not on subcommittee sometimes request and are always granted an opportunity to testify.

The most readily available set of witnesses was the Legislative Action Committee of the U. S. Conference of Mayors, a bipartisan group headed by Mayor John Lindsay of New York (then a Republican), and including Mayor Richard Daley of Chicago, the most influential local Democratic politician in America. This committee grew out of a special meeting of big-city mayors called by Mayor James Tate of Philadelphia during the annual conference of the National League of Cities the previous November. At that time rumors were floating that President Nixon planned to veto the Employment and Manpower Act, and the mayors got together to mobilize support against a veto. They sent John Gunther, executive director of the U. S. Conference of Mayors, to see OMB Director George Shultz, but Gunther and the mayors were no more persuasive than anybody else in convincing Shultz, and through him the President, that the bill should not be vetoed.

These leading mayors met again in December to form the Legislative Action Committee, which adopted jobs as number one priority. Then they went into cities around the country, holding hearings in order to publicize urban problems and to build support for national legislation. So the mayors' committee was a ready-made group for the Senate hearings, and Senator Nelson invited them to the first hearing on February 8. They followed the opening witness, Warren B. Magnuson of Washington, an influential member of the Senate Appropriations Committee who was deeply concerned about high unemployment in the Seattle area, where there had been massive layoffs in the aerospace industry.

Altogether, the Senate Subcommittee on Employment, Manpower and Poverty conducted four days of hearings, between February 8 and 24, and heard the following witnesses:

February   8: Senator Warren G. Magnuson of Washington
                Nine mayors representing the U. S. Conference of Mayors

February 17: Three county officials representing the National Association of Counties
                A spokesman for the National Farmers Union
                A rural community-action director

February 23: Secretary of Labor James D. Hodgson and Assistant Secretary Malcolm R. Lovell, Jr.

February 24: Three black members of the House of Representatives
                Three governors, lined up through the National Governors Conference
                Senator Phillip Hart of Michigan

In addition, the subcommittee received and published statements or letters from the AFL-CIO, two labor unions (public employees; oil and chemical workers), two professional associations (solid wastes; park and recreation), and a representative of Indian tribes. All the witnesses and statement writers except Hodgson and Lovell favored enactment of S. 31, and most of them had specific suggestions for changes in the bill.[1]

Since senators serve on numerous subcommittees, attendance at hearings is often low, and Subcommittee Chairman Nelson was the only Democrat present during three of the four hearings; but on the opening day, when the nine mayors appeared, he was joined by four of six other Democrats on the subcommittee. On the Republican side, Javits and Schweiker of Pennsylvania attended three hearings, Taft was there twice, and Bob Packwood of Oregon, a member of the full committee but not the subcommittee, was present at the first hearing. Of the Republicans, Javits and Taft were the most active in questioning witnesses. Two Democrats and two Republicans missed all four hearings.

The appearance of Hodgson and Lovell on February 23 marked the opening skirmish of 1971 between Congress and the administration in the battle for employment and manpower legislation. Hodgson opposed the Emergency Employment Act because it was not in keeping with a set of programs outlined by President Nixon in his January state-of-the-union address. The President's programs included four recommendations related to this issue: (1) a federal budget with an anticipated deficit of $11 billion to stimulate the national economy; (2) general revenue sharing, which in its first full year would provide $5 billion in unrestricted funds to state and local governments; (3) a $4-billion welfare-reform measure, including a basic level of income support and public-service jobs as a device for getting people off welfare rolls; and (4) a manpower revenue-sharing proposal. The first was a new twist in the economic game plan, and the second and third were carried over from the last Congress, but the fourth was something new.

In his state-of-the-union message the President had proclaimed "a new American revolution" consisting of reorganization of the executive branch and modification of intergovernmental finance by instituting general revenue sharing and special revenue sharing for four fields: manpower, education, urban community development, and rural development.[2]

Special revenue sharing represented a further development of thinking beyond the block-grant approach to reducing the number of federal categorical programs. Under both approaches, categorical programs would be consolidated and their funds placed in a single money pool for each field. To receive a block grant, state and local governments would have to submit comprehensive plans and budgets before the administering federal agency would release funds. Under special revenue sharing, in contrast, funds would be allocated by formula to state and local governments, which could spend them as they chose for activities in the particular field without prior federal approval but subject to a federal post-audit for legal conformity. The administration's manpower-reform measure of 1969 and 1970 utilized the block-grant approach, and its new proposal called for manpower special-revenue sharing.

Unfortunately, Secretary Hodgson could not tell the subcommittee much about the specifics of manpower revenue sharing because the administration had not yet completed its draft of a bill. Senator Nelson pointed out that the proposed Emergency Employment Act embraced the idea of temporary public-service employment, which the President had endorsed in his veto message, and had even used a trigger mechanism patterned after the administration's previous manpower-reform proposal. Hodgson replied that "you would find yourself thinking that you have come to play ball in our court and we have moved the court." This is true, he acknowledged, "because we have moved on to what might be called a macro-objective in manpower programming tied to general revenue sharing. We are thinking of not just a mere change or simple revision of the traditional approach, but a real major change—a whole conceptual change." Senator Javits asked him whether the President would veto an emergency-employment bill which was not part of special revenue sharing. Hodgson replied, "I would think there are strong possibilities that he would."[3]

At the hearing, Secretary Hodgson asked Senator Nelson to wait for the manpower revenue-sharing bill and to consider it before taking action on emergency-employment legislation. Nelson responded that the need for immediate action on the jobs front was too great and that, furthermore, the subcommittee had to take up the Economic Opportunity Act next because it was scheduled to expire on June 30. Accordingly, the Nelson subcommittee moved ahead to mark-up of S. 31 and sent it on for further consideration by the full committee. The Labor and Public Welfare Committee was now under the chairmanship of Harrison A. Williams, Jr. of New Jersey.

The mark-up sessions kept the basic substance of the original bill, but made a number of revisions, including a statement of intent to move participants into other employment and training. The committee bill tied down the authorization, which had been left open in the original, to $750 million for the 1972 fiscal year and $1 billion for fiscal 1973. The committee approved the bill on March 17 by a vote of 15 to 2. Ten Democrats and five Republicans favored the measure, and two Republicans opposed it, but the five affirmative Republicans reserved the right to work for an accommodation with the manpower revenue-sharing bill.

They could make that statement because on March 6 the administration bill had finally arrived in Congress, where it was introduced in the Senate by Senator Prouty (with three Republican cosponsors) and in the House by Representative Quie (with nine other Republicans).[4] According to this bill, manpower revenue sharing would replace the Manpower Development and Training Act and the manpower provisions of the Economic Opportunity Act but would allow state and local governments to continue whatever elements of those programs they wished. To get the money, these governmental units would have to adopt an annual program statement in advance, but the contents would not be reviewed by the Department of Labor before releasing the funds. Among the eligible programs would be "transitional public-service employment," and the bill also contained a trigger mechanism to increase training and employment funds by 10 percent when national unemployment rose above 4.5 percent. The bill had no specific dollar figure for authorization, but the President's budget earmarked $2 billion for this program, an amount one-third above the current manpower funding level in the two acts to be replaced. Presumably, the $600-million increase would go for public-service employment.

But this bill was put aside as the Democrats prepared for floor action on emergency employment. Once a bill is approved by committee, its staff still has to prepare a committee report, and it is usually a week or more before the committee can file its report to the Senate. The committee report on S. 31 was filed on March 27.[5] By Senate rules, a bill may be taken up the next day after the committee report on it is filed, but the precise schedule is determined by the majority leader (in this case, Mike Mansfield of Montana). Since the Democratic leadership wanted quick action, Mansfield scheduled the Emergency Employment Act for immediate consideration, and the bill came up for debate on April 1.[6]

Senators Nelson and Javits teamed up to provide floor leadership. Each made opening statements to present the case for the legislation, and Javits, as the ranking minority member, summarized the administration's opposing views. Their major floor support came from Alan Cranston, a Democrat from California. Dominick, who had voted against the bill in committee, led the opposition, stating that this was just another categorical program and one which would feature "make-work" and the use of government as the "employer of last resort." He was joined by Taft, who had also voted "no" in committee, and by Robert P. Griffin, a Republican from Michigan.

The key vote came on a motion by Senator Prouty to recommit the bill to committee, with a requirement to report back by May 4. Prouty argued that recommittal would give the subcommittee time to incorporate transitional public-service employment into a comprehensive manpower act. Nelson replied that such a schedule could not be met because the subcommittee was already at work considering the administration's request for legislation on an extension of the Economic Opportunity Act. The Prouty motion lost by a vote of 44 to 29. Only four Democrats, all southerners, joined Prouty, and seven Republicans voted against the motion.

Once the recommittal motion was disposed of, the Senate took up several amendments to the bill. Proposals by Taft to remove the minimum-wage requirement and to place a ceiling on salaries were both defeated, and so was a Dominick amendment to have the program terminate when and if manpower revenue sharing started. However, Nelson and Javits accepted Dominick's proposal that the word "transitional" be added at six places in the bill, an amendment which Dominick had drafted with assistance from the Labor Department, and also a Taft amendment deleting provisions for retirement benefits. Three other minor amendments were approved. The final vote was 62 to 10. Dominick, seven other conservative Republicans, and two southern Democrats represented the hard-core opposition, but Taft, Griffin, and Prouty voted for final passage. So in one afternoon the Senate adopted S. 31, the Emergency Employment Act.

By this time, the House Labor and Education Committee had completed its hearings and was marking up its version of emergency-employment legislation. The House committee had experienced several changes in personnel since the previous Congress. Dominick Daniels, chairman of the Select Subcommittee on Labor, had taken full command of manpower legislation when James O'Hara dropped off this subcommittee to become chairman of another subcommittee. At the same time, Subcommittee Counsel Daniel Krivit had taken over staff responsibility for manpower bills, when O'Hara's man, Jim Harrison, moved to the other subcommittee. But Austin Sullivan, legislative aide to Representative Carl Perkins of Kentucky, chairman of the full committee, continued to be involved, as he had been in past manpower legislation. On the Republican side, Albert Quie had replaced William Ayres (who had been defeated at the polls) as the ranking minority member of the full committee, and Marvin L. Esch of Michigan had become ranking Republican on the Select Subcommittee on Labor, where William Steiger remained as an influential member. Minority staff responsibility had shifted from Michael Bernstein to Charles Radcliffe.

At the start of its hearings, the Daniels subcommittee had three bills to consider, i.e., those introduced by Perkins, O'Hara, and Daniels. The Perkins bill (H. R. 17) authorized $4.7 billion for emergency-employment assistance over a four-year period; many of its provisions were taken from the vetoed Employment and Manpower Act of 1970. The O'Hara bill (H. R. 29) contained an open-ended authorization to pay the costs of agreements with federal, state, and local governmental agencies to provide useful public-service employment to unemployed persons. The Daniels bill (H. R. 3613) was similar to Senator Nelson's bill (S. 31) except that it set up a five-year program rather than the two-year program in the Senate version, had specific dollar figures instead of open-ended authorization, and a few minor differences. The similarities occurred not because of any direct collaboration in drafting (representatives and senators do not ordinarily confer at this stage of legislation) but because Daniels and Krivit recognized that the Nelson bill was a good point of departure for the House. Moreover, Kenneth Young, the AFL-CIO lobbyist, was in touch with both sides of Congress and had acted as an intermediary.

By coincidence, the first House hearing was on the last day of the Senate hearings on emergency-employment legislation, and the last day of House hearings occurred on the day the Senate Labor and Public Welfare Committee voted to report its bill. As in the Senate, witness selection in the House is controlled by the subcommittee chairman, but he is receptive to suggestions from other members, including the minority. One decision is whether to call witnesses from the administration first, last, or in between. For administration-proposed legislation, they usually come first, but when legislative initiative comes from the Congress, they often appear later. In this case, Daniels invited the secretary of labor to appear at the first hearing, but Hodgson declined this and two subsequent dates because the administration was still working on its manpower proposal. He finally came on March 17, the day after the administration's manpower revenue-sharing bill was introduced in Congress.

Altogether, the Daniels subcommittee held six days of hearings with the following witnesses:[7]

February 24: Two governors who were in Washington attending a meeting of the National Governors Conference

February 25: Four mayors representing the U. S. Conference of Mayors and the National League of Cities

March 2: Representative Charles E. Bennett of Florida
Two economics professors

March 3: A spokesman for a national conservation organization
A social scientist who had studied public-service employment

March 4: Two people from the National Rural Electric Cooperative Association
Two county officials representing the National Association of Counties
Representative Robert N. C. Nix of Pennsylvania

March 17: Secretary of Labor James D. Hodgson, Assistant Secretary Malcolm R. Lovell, Jr., and Manpower Administrator Paul J. Fasser, Jr.
Representative Shirley Chisholm of New York

Also included in the hearings record were letters and written statements submitted by a mayor, a governor, the AFL-CIO, a public-employees union, a farm organization, a day-care organization, a solid-waste-management association, and the Chamber of Commerce of the United States. Thus, the subcommittee heard the views of different levels of government, rural interests, business and labor, professional associations and academic scholars, members of Congress, and officials from the Executive Branch.

Although most of the witnesses favored public-service employment, a greater diversity of views was expressed than at the Senate hearings. Governor Calvin L. Rampton of Utah, a Democrat, was solidly behind public-service employment, but he wanted to make it a permanent program which would continue to serve disadvantaged persons and not be linked to a trigger mechanism. Governor John A. Love of Colorado, a Republican, agreed that the program should be permanent, but he wanted the jobs themselves to be transitional. The spokesmen for rural areas recommended provisions to assure that rural America got its fair share of the jobs. Representative Bennett, who was not a member of the Labor and Education Committee, spoke on behalf of his own bill (H. R. 2144), which provided for public-service jobs to be filled from a register of unemployed persons maintained by the Department of Labor. The U. S. Chamber of Commerce asked the subcommittee to defer emergency-employment legislation and to consider the administration's manpower revenue-sharing measure instead. All the other witnesses, except for those from the administration, supported emergency-job legislation, although some of them proposed changes in matters of detail.

All eleven Democrats of the subcommittee attended at least one of the six hearings and so did five of the seven Republicans. (Members of the House have fewer subcommittee assignments than senators do.) In addition, Representative Quie, ranking minority member of the full committee and an ex officio member of all subcommittees, participated in three hearings. Greatest attendance was on the last day, when the secretary of labor appeared and twelve of the eighteen members plus Quie were in attendance. Only Chairman Daniels and Representative Esch, the ranking minority member of the subcommittee, were at all six hearings, but on the Republican side Steiger and Forsythe were present five times. Daniels and Esch were the most persistent questioners of witnesses, although

Democrat Hawkins was a major participant in the three hearings he attended. Compared to Republican senators, the minority members of the House were much more aggressive in searching for flaws in the proposed legislation. Representative Esch in particular, assisted by Steiger, pursued a line of questioning designed to build a case for the administration's view that transitional public-service employment should be a part of comprehensive manpower legislation and should not be handled in a separate bill. But they could not do much to promote the administration's manpower revenue-sharing proposal during the first five days of hearings because it had not yet been introduced.

The day after this bill went to Congress, Secretary of Labor Hodgson, Assistant Secretary Lovell, and Manpower Administrator Paul Fasser appeared before the Daniels subcommittee. In his testimony, Hodgson repeated much of what he had told the Senate subcommittee: that the administration wanted manpower revenue sharing to go along with welfare reform, general revenue sharing, and stimulation of the economy through a federal budget deficit, but that transitional public-service employment was acceptable as part of manpower revenue-sharing and welfare reform. He criticized the Perkins, O'Hara, and Daniels bills in the following manner:

> In the administration's view, there are two principal deficiencies of these bills. First, they are not part of a thorough reorganization and reform of our manpower programs. Second, and most importantly, they do not adequately and unequivocally assure that such public-service employment positions would indeed be transitional and committed to developing manpower skills. All bills do contain provisions which would encourage skill training or ultimate placement in nonsubsidized employment. But they do not require it. And they do not provide an adequate administrative mechanism to enforce such encouragement.[8]

Esch and Steiger asked the secretary a series of questions designed to build the case that public-service employment was merely another categorical program which would detract from achieving overall reform. At one point Steiger asked: "Are you saying that, were the committee to recommend one of the three public service employment programs before us, you would actively oppose it?" And Hodgson replied: "We would indeed have to oppose it, yes."[9]

This answer excited Daniels, who remarked: "The Chair would like to state that during this past year the legislation considered by this committee has always met with the threat of a veto, and I want to state publicly that I resent such threats."[10]

With the battlelines thus drawn, the Daniels subcommittee held mark-up sessions on April 21 and 22 and reported an amended version of the Daniels bill (H. R. 3613) to the full committee. On April 27, the Committee on Education and Labor made further amendments and approved the bill by a vote of 23 to 10, with one Republican joining the twenty-two Democrats in the affirmative.

The major change made in committee was the addition of a special employment-assistance fund to direct job money to areas where unemployment had exceeded 6 percent for three consecutive months. This idea, first set forth in embryonic form in the Perkins bill, was refined by the time mark-up sessions began. It became Section 6 of the bill, while the regular program was described in Section 5. The committee authorized $250 million for the special-employment-assistance fund for each of the next four years, and for the regular program $200 million immediately, $750 million in the next fiscal year (1972), and $1 million in each of the three years following. The committee also made several other changes in the bill but did not alter its fundamental principles or yield to the administration's objections to a bill separate from comprehensive manpower reform.

At this stage, Congresswoman Edith Green of Oregon became an important supporter of emergency employment. She had opposed the bipartisan manpower bill in the previous session because it diminished the role of vocational-education agencies and enhanced community-action agencies. In this session, she supported legislation producing jobs with the issue of manpower reorganization removed. Her support was valuable because she maintained cordial relations not only with Daniels but also with more conservative southern Democrats, with whom she was sometimes allied on fiscal matters.

During the mark-up sessions of both the subcommittee and full committee, the Republicans attempted unsuccessfully to substitute the President's proposal for manpower special-revenue sharing. They also failed to place a two-year limitation on participation. As a result, the Republicans, with the exception of Ogden Reid of New York (a liberal who would later switch to the Democratic Party), filed minority views. They repeated the arguments made at the hearings for comprehensive legislation and quoted from the testimony developed in response to their questions. And they criticized various details of the Democrats' bill, claiming in particular that it failed to make proper provision for transition to unsupported employment.[11]

Before the emergency-employment bill could go to the House floor for consideration, it had to pass through the Rules Committee, which is responsible for regulating the order of business on the floor of the House and for prescribing the length and manner of debate. This process is known as "giving a rule."

On May 11, Perkins and Daniels appeared before the Rules Committee, accompanied by Mrs. Green. Quie and Esch were there to represent the minority. Perkins requested and the Rules Committee granted a rule providing for three hours of debate on H. R. 3613 as reported by the Labor and Education Committee, after which amendments to the bill would be in order. The Republicans asked that the rule permit a House vote on the motion to substitute the text of H. R. 8141 for the committee bill in its entirety; this was a bill which Esch had introduced as a slightly revised version of the manpower revenue-sharing bill. The Rules Committee, however, turned down Esch's request by a vote of 8 to 7, with negative votes coming from two conservative southern Democrats and the five Republicans on the committee.

When the emergency-employment legislation became the order of business on May 18, the House first had to vote on the resolution from the Rules Committee. Republican strategy was to modify the rule in order to allow a vote on H. R. 8141. They succeeded in gaining all but five Republican votes and in obtaining sufficient support from southern Democrats to win procedural votes, 210 to 182 and 211 to 172.[12] This occurred because two southern Democrats, William M. Colmer of Mississippi, chairman of the Rules Committee, and Joe D. Waggonner of Lousiana, had worked out a deal to enlist southern votes in exchange for Republican support in opposing legislation to strengthen the Equal Employment Commission, a measure about to come up for consideration.

Most legislative debate in the House of Representatives occurs when the body transforms itself into the Committee of the Whole House on the State of Union. When it does this, the House operates under less rigid rules than those of the House in regular session and requires that only a hundred members be present for a quorum, rather than a majority. Accordingly, after the final vote on the rule, the House resolved itself into the Committee of the Whole for three hours of debate on emergency-employment legislation, with half the time controlled by Daniels as floor manager, and half by Quie as leader of the opposition. The opening debate lasted an hour and then the Committee of the Whole rose in late afternoon of May 18 and did not return to consideration of the bill until June 1.

The delay occurred because the Democrats had not been able to keep their ranks intact during the votes on adoption of the rule, and they did not want to risk continued defections which might lead to a House vote in favor of the Republican substitute. The Democrats needed more time to line up support for assured passage of the emergency-employment bill. Perkins, assisted by Speaker Albert, Majority Leader Hale Boggs of Louisiana, and Wilbur D. Mills of Arkansas, chairman of the Ways and Means Committee, worked on winning over southern votes. Legislative representatives from the AFL-CIO, the National League of Cities/U. S. Conference of Mayors, the American Vocational Association, and the Leadership Conference on Civil Rights also participated in the effort to secure support for the bill. By the end of May the Democrats were ready, and the House resumed consideration of the legislation on the first two days in June.

Since the stage was set for a vote on the Republican substitute of a manpower revenue-sharing bill in place of the Democrats' emergency-employment bill, most of the three days of debate—May 18 and June 1 and 2 — centered on the relative merits of the two proposals.[13] The Republicans conceded that a well-thought-out public-service employment program was desirable and claimed that this would be possible under their bill, a measure which would also accomplish manpower reform. They repeated their previous argument against the emergency-employment bill as being another categorical program. The Democrats argued that manpower revenue sharing would not create the new jobs needed immediately for Vietnam veterans and other unemployed persons but would merely rearrange existing programs. They further maintained that the Republican bill had not been heard in committee, that it omitted safeguards on the use of funds, and that the Department of Labor was not even able to state how the money would be allocated to states and localities. The main thrust of the debate had the Democrats attacking and Republicans defending manpower revenue sharing, with neither side considering the merits and details of the emergency-employment bill.

Perkins and Daniels carried the main load of the substantive argument for the Democrats, with assistance from Roman C. Pucinski of Illinois, who repeatedly directed questions to the Republicans. The Democrats orchestrated their attack and defense so that on the third day of debate major statements were made by three leading members of the Labor and Education Committee whose views carried weight with different segments of the Democratic Party in the House: Hawkins, a member of the Black Caucus; O'Hara, an acknowledged manpower expert and a leading liberal; and Mrs. Green, a middle-of-the-road, rather independent Democrat who was sometimes allied with the southerners. Twenty-three other Democrats spoke in favor of the committee bill, including Speaker Albert and Majority Leader Boggs. Reid was the lone Republican to register support for the emergency-employment bill and opposition to manpower revenue sharing.

Quie, Esch, and Steiger were most prominent on the Republican side, but eight other Republicans spoke out for manpower revenue sharing. This support included a strong statement by John N. Erlenborn of Illinois on the third day of debate and a brief comment by Minority Leader Gerald R. Ford of Michigan toward the end of the proceedings.

At the end of three hours of debate, Esch offered H. R. 8141 as a substitute for the committee bill. It was during this phase of the debate that Green, Albert, and Boggs made their statements against manpower revenue sharing, and John B. Anderson of Illinois, representing Republican leadership, spoke in favor. In a teller vote taken as members walked between clerks recording yes and no votes, the motion lost, 204 to 182. Manpower revenue sharing had been rejected.

Immediately, Esch offered an amendment to the committee bill to permit no individual to remain in public-service employment longer than two years, but this was defeated by a voice vote. No more amendments were presented, and the committee bill was approved forthwith by a voice vote. Whereupon the Committee of the Whole rose, and the House returned to its more formal procedures. Steiger then moved that the emergency-employment bill (H. R. 3613) be recommitted to the Labor and Education Committee, but the motion lost by a vote of 201 to 183. This vote and the one against substituting H. R. 8141 in the Committee of the Whole were the crucial votes, and they showed that Perkins, the House leadership, and allied lobbyists had been able to change twenty-five to thirty votes between May 18 and June 2. This effort, not oratory on the House floor, made the difference.

With the test issues out of the way, 244 members voted for the emergency-employment bill on final passage, and 142 voted in the negative. The House then substituted its measure for the language of the Senate-passed bill, S. 31, and requested a conference with the Senate. The Speaker immediately appointed a prearranged group of conferees, twelve Democrats and eight Republicans. A week later the presiding officer of the Senate appointed the seven Democrats and five Republicans on the Subcommitee on Employment, Manpower, and Poverty to represent the Senate on the conference committee.

When the conference met on June 15, members found they had forty differences to reconcile, compared to only half a dozen in the versions originally introduced by Nelson and Daniels. For proponents of public-service employment, the House bill was stronger than the Senate bill and was scheduled to run five years rather than two. The Democratic representatives appointed to the conference, having stood firm and kept their bill intact through the House proceedings, were in no mood to compromise. All spring administration spokesmen had been threatening a presidential veto, and after the December veto of the manpower bill, congressional Democrats were more willing to believe that this was no idle threat. They felt that since a veto was probably inevitable, they should keep the bill strong in order to gain maximum political advantage from their attempt to deal with continuing high unemployment. Republican conferees, too, expected a presidential veto. In this atmosphere, the first conference meeting made little progress.

But behind the scenes, changes had been occurring within the Nixon administration. On December 10, the day the Employment and Manpower Act of 1970 passed conference and six days before the President's veto, Nixon had told a news conference:

> I believe our economic policies are working. First, we have cooled off the inflation. It is beginning to recede, the rate of inflation.
>
> Second, we are now moving into the second half of our plan of expanding our fiscal policy and that, together with an expanded monetary supply, we believe will move the economy up.[14]

His optimism was not shared by Arthur F. Burns, whom Nixon had appointed chairman of the Federal Reserve Board the previous February. Only three days before the President's news conference, Burns, in a speech at Pepperdine College in Los Angeles, had expressed his concern about continuing inflation and had suggested ten specific remedies, including establishment of a high-level price-and-wage review board.[15] As inflation continued undiminished, Burns' predictions were proven correct, and by spring all seven members of the Federal Reserve Board of Governors concurred with his recommendation of an "incomes policy."

By then Paul McCracken and Hendrik Houthakker of the Council of Economic Advisers were also leaning in that direction, but Herbert Stein, the third member of the council, opposed this kind of governmental intervention. George Shultz was also strongly against controls, and he more than anybody else seemed to have the President's ear. John Connally, who became secretary of the treasury in

February, 1971, a politician rather than an economist, was more pragmatic than ideological, but as a conservative he was certainlv not oriented toward economic regulation by government. John Ehrlichman, closest to the President on domestic matters, was more-or-less neutral. Nixon himself, on the basis of his experience in the Office of Price Administration during World War II and for basic ideological reasons, was not favorably disposed toward government controls. But the administration was definitely in a state of uncertainty which continued until mid-August, when Nixon announced a wage-and-price freeze.

The news on the employment front was no better. In five of the six months between December, 1970, and May, 1971, the unemployment rate was 6 percent or higher, and it showed no sign of going down as had been expected according to the economic game plan. This was becoming a major political problem for the administration. The Democrats were pressing hard on the unemployment issue, congressional Republicans were becoming restive, and the 1972 presidential and congressional elections loomed on the horizon.

On June 15, when the emergency-employment conference first met, Congress completed action on a $2-billion accelerated public-works bill, which the President opposed and planned to veto. The emergency-employment act would soon follow, and Nixon did not want to block two job-creation bills in close succession. Neither Nixon nor his close political and economic advisers—Ehrlichman, Shultz, and the others — had much enthusiasm for subsidized employment, but the President concluded that a program of public-service jobs at this time was the least "evil" of the measures that the Democrats in Congress might possibly produce. So political pragmatism more than carefully conceived economic policy led the administration to reconsider its position on the emergency-employment bill.

Accordingly, White House staff instructed Undersecretary of Labor Laurence H. Silberman to explore whether an accommodation was possible on this legislation. Silberman got in touch with the conference leaders shortly after the first unproductive session of the conference committee. When he appeared on the scene, they sensed that a compromise was in the offing because many of them had dealt with him the year before in working out an occupational health-and-safety act, and they knew him to be one of the administration's top political operators.

Democratic and Republican conferees held a series of informal meetings in the Capitol with Silberman, Lovell, and other Labor Department personnel. Lobbyists from the AFL-CIO and the League of Cities/U. S. Conference of Mayors were also heavily involved in the negotiations. The key provision for the administration was the "transitional" language which Senator Dominick had gotten into the bill when it was before the Senate. This was hard for the House Democrats to swallow, but they did so when they saw they might get the House Republican conferees to sign the conference report. Thereafter, other compromises fell into place.

Perkins, Hawkins, and other representatives got the special Section 6 program for their districts, which had quite high unemployment rates. Since the 1971 fiscal year was nearly over, the conference committee dropped the $200 million authorized immediately by the House, agreed upon $750 million for fiscal 1972 and $1 billion for fiscal 1973 for the regular program (Section 5) and $250 million for each of those years for the Section 6 program, and omitted provisions for the fourth and fifth year of the House bill. To seal the agreement with the administration, both Senator Nelson and Representative Daniels promised prompt hearings on manpower-reform legislation, including the administration's special-revenue-sharing proposal. (In fact, Nelson had already held one hearing in order to take testimony from Secretary of Labor Hodgson.)

All members of the conference committee signed a joint explanatory statement except Senator Dominick, who had refused to participate in the conference proceedings.[16] This statement took great pains to spell out the meaning of "transitional" public-service employment. "Transitional," the statement indicated, meant, first, that the act was to expire in two years and that funds for the regular program would cease to be obligated when the national unemployment rate fell below 4.5 percent and, second, that public-service employment jobs were intended to lead, whenever possible, to public and private jobs not supported by the act. However, the word "transitional" did not limit the length of time any individual could stay on a specific job, did not limit the kind of jobs available to temporary jobs (thus teaching, police, nursing, and fire protection jobs were eligible), and did not prohibit the reemployment of persons laid off regular public-service jobs because of local fiscal problems. From this perspective, "transitional" was a more rhetorical device to make the bill palatable to the President than a restriction on program participation.

But from the administration's perspective, this language and the considerable flexibility built into the compromise bill would provide sufficient administrative latitude. President Nixon confirmed his acceptance of the conference version of the Emergency Employment Act in this veto message on the public-works bill. He stated:

> Expansion of job opportunities for those presently unemployed is one of this administration's highest priorities. Measures to expand job opportunities must be effective; they must hold real promise of providing the jobs when they are needed, where they are needed, for the persons who most need them.[17]

The President said that the emergency-employment bill adopted by the conference committee met this test. In contrast, he indicated that the accelerated public-works bill did not because construction projects require a long lead time, provide most jobs in the construction industry (which already was experiencing rapid cost inflation), and would not provide many jobs for Vietnam veterans, unskilled youth, and other persons unemployed because of lack of training.

This public-works veto message reached Congress the morning of June 29, and toward the end of that afternoon the Senate adopted the conference report. Proceedings on the Senate floor consisted mainly of a colloquy between Nelson and Javits on what the conference committee had decided, with supporting speeches by Senators Cranston and Williams. However, Dominick made one last attack on the program as being, in his view, the start of a permanent federal subsidy of permanent jobs in state and local government. He was joined in opposition by ten other hard-core conservatives when the Senate adopted the conference report by a vote of 75 to 11.[18]

When the House took up the report on July 1, Perkins described how the conferees had worked out their differences, and Daniels and Green endorsed the conference bill. Quie, Esch, and Steiger explained how the bill had been improved to make it acceptable to them. Only H. R. Gross, a Republican from Iowa, long a foe of federal spending, spoke in opposition to the $2.25-billion program. But not many sided with him in the 343 to 14 vote for adoption of the conference report.[19]

Now all that was required was the President's signature. After the bill was engrossed, it was sent to the White House. Nixon signed it on July 12 at his home in San Clemente, California. The political importance of the measure can be noted in his remarks at the time:

> I think it is particularly significant that I am able to sign this bill and have the opportunity to comment upon it in California. . . . It will be particularly helpful in areas like California, which has higher than the national average of unemployment due to lay-offs in aerospace and related defense industries.[20]

And with that, a two-year public-service employment program became law.

4

CHOOSING THE
BENEFICIARIES

Although the fact is seldom well enough articulated to enable the
general public to grasp precisely what is occurring, Congress and
the Executive Branch are arbiters in the distribution of national
resources. Legislative and executive decisions determine how much
of the national income is absorbed by federal taxes and how that tax
burden is assigned. Congress and the President, between them, decide how federal funds are spent—which programs are funded and
how much they receive. Their decisions affect which individuals,
groups, and geographical areas benefit from federal programs. The
basic legislation provides guidance about beneficiaries, and for each
grant-in-aid program, Congress adopts criteria for allocating funds
among states and localities. But usually the administering agency
has some discretion in deciding how to apply the congressional man-
date. These decisions by Congress and executive officials are political acts which determine who gets what, when, and how.

Such political decisions were made in the course of adopting the
Emergency Employment Act and implementing its provisions in
the Public Employment Program. Congress decided what people
and which geographic areas would benefit. As Congress appropriated funds and as the Nixon administration got the new program
into operation other decisions about beneficiaries were made.

One set of decisions which Congress made affected what individuals and groups would be hired for emergency employment. The
original bills introduced by Senator Nelson (S.31) and Representative Daniels (H. R. 3613) indicated (in identical language) that the

46

program was directed to the unemployed and the underemployed. //
Among such persons, the bills established no priorities, but the general statement of findings and purpose identified low-income persons, youth, recently discharged veterans, and persons affected by technological change and shifts in federal expenditures (such as in defense, aerospace, and construction industries) as groups needing assistance through public-service employment. Thus, the legislation was written to appeal to a broad array of interests.

Since the funds authorized in the bill were insufficient by far to ||
provide jobs for all the unemployed, priorities would eventually have to be expressed—by law, regulation, or by the aggregate of individual hiring decisions made by local and state governments. In an effort to provide guidance, the Senate Labor and Public Welfare Committee amended the bill with a clause requiring the secretary of labor to make the public-service jobs available equitably to different segments of the unemployed in each segment. The committee also amended the general-findings-and-purpose clause to list these segments, and nearly a third of the committee report was given over to a more detailed description of who they were: workers laid off in aerospace, defense, and construction industries, unemployed veterans, older workers, migrants, persons of limited English-speaking ability, persons receiving welfare assistance, and Indians.[1]

When the bill reached the Senate floor, Senator Taft offered an amendment to set a maximum salary of $600 per month (no limit was stipulated in the bill) in order "to take care of those truly in need and not those with skills they can take elsewhere."[2] But the sentiment in the Senate was that unemployed engineers, technicians and other skilled persons should be considered for jobs at pay commensurate with their skills, and the amendment was defeated. In the debate, Taft lamented the lack of a veterans-preference clause, but he did not offer an amendment to add one.

But on the House side, veterans got more attention. Republican members of the Education and Labor Committee became their champion and offered an amendment to provide preference for Vietnam veterans. In response, Subcommittee Chairman Daniels conferred with Representative Olin E. Teague of Texas, chairman of the Veterans' Affairs Committee, to work out appropriate language: "unemployed and underemployed persons who served in the Armed Forces in Indochina on or after August 5, 1964" (the day Congress passed the Gulf of Tonkin resolution authorizing U. S. military involvement in Indochina). On a motion by Representative Edith Green, "Korea" was added.

The House Labor Committee also placed a ceiling of $12,000 on participants' salaries to be paid from federal funds (localities could pay more with their own funds), and it added a restriction that not more than a third of the participants could be professionals, though this did not apply to classroom teachers.[3] These provisions, which became part of the House-passed bill, constituted a compromise between those who wanted the program to be directed toward persons in greatest need and those who wanted unemployed persons with technical and professional skills also to benefit.

In the conference committee, the Senate conferees accepted the House's limitations on hiring professionals and the maximum salary. The veterans' clause was changed from "preference" to "special consideration," and the conference report stated: "The conferees strongly urged the secretary of labor to ensure that all possible efforts are made to assure the equitable employment of returning veterans in public service programs."[4]

The conference committee eliminated the Senate's language on equitable distribution of public-service jobs among different segments of the unemployed but retained the broad listing of prospective beneficiaries, including disadvantaged persons, youth, older persons, veterans, welfare recipients, and persons displaced by technological change. Congress as a whole accepted the conference bill.

One other congressional decision related to beneficiaries. The two major bills as introduced permitted 15 percent of the funds to go for training and manpower services. The Senate committee raised this to 20 percent but placed a limitation of 1 percent for evaluation expenses. The House committee stuck with the 15 percent maximum for training and manpower services and added a clause requiring that not less than 85 percent of federal funds go for wages and employment benefits of persons employed in public-service jobs. These House provisions and the Senate limitation on evaluation prevailed in conference. The net effect was that program participants would receive most of the funds in wages and fringe benefits and that not much would be available for the salaries of administrators, counselors, teachers, and other professional personnel.

A second set of congressional decisions related to the distribution of funds among the states and local areas. The original Nelson and Daniels bills had a fairly simple clause requiring the secretary of labor to apportion funds "among States and local areas within each State on an equitable basis, and to the extent practicable such funds shall be apportioned in proportion to the unemployment in each area."[5]

As the legislative process moved along, Senator Nelson became concerned about rural areas in his state of Wisconsin, which had a high unemployment rate even though the number of unemployed persons was relatively small compared to big cities. Other senators shared this concern, and some wondered about Indian reservations. Consequently the Senate Labor Committee kept the phrase "equitable basis" as the standard for apportionment but specified rural areas, urban areas, and Indian reservations as local areas to be considered. Then the committee added that both "the relative numbers of unemployed persons and the severity of unemployment in each such area" should be taken into account.[6] The severity factor would benefit not only rural areas with high rates of unemployment but also urban areas which were suffering high unemployment because of cutbacks in aerospace and defense budgets. The Senate accepted these provisions when it passed the bill.

The House Labor Committee took a somewhat different tack. Chairman Perkins, from a district in Eastern Kentucky with a perennially high unemployment rate, introduced an employment bill authorizing $4.7 billion for a four-year period for public-service employment. This bill provided that if the national unemployment rate dropped below 4 percent for three consecutive months during this period, the leftover funds would be transferred to a special fund in the Treasury to serve specific areas where unemployment remained above 4 percent. During subcommittee hearings, Representative Hawkins, from the Watts area of Los Angeles, and other Congressmen from low-income, inner-city districts expressed concern about unemployment rates in their districts, rates much higher than for the cities as a whole. Representative Daniels and committee staff responded by taking the special-fund idea of the Perkins bill and establishing a specific appropriation for local areas with unemployment over 6 percent. This was expressed in a new Section 6, which Daniels presented successfully at the subcommittee mark-up session.

For the regular program authorized by Section 5, the House committee provided that at least 80 percent of the money would be apportioned among the states equitably, taking into consideration the number of unemployed, but that no state would receive less than $1.5 million. Within each state, such funds would also be apportioned by taking into consideration the number of unemployed. The secretary of labor would have discretion on how to allocate the remaining 20 percent of Section 5 funds. The House accepted these provisions for Sections 5 and 6.

In the conference committee, the House conferees, reflecting their district orientation, were strongly committed to provisions for a special program for areas of high unemployment. Senate conferees were sympathetic to this concern and accepted Section 6. When the bill had been before the House, Representative Steiger had objected to the creation of a special fund in the Treasury, and in order to effect a compromise with the Republicans, the Democratic majority agreed to drop this provision. With areas of high unemployment taken care of, the Senate conferees "receded" from the language requiring severity of unemployment to be taken into account in apportioning funds and accepted the House's wording on Section 5 funds. The conference report strongly indicated that subareas of high unemployment within cities and counties would be eligible for Section 6 projects.

Compared with the bills introduced in January, the conference bill adopted by the two houses in June reflected a shift toward areas of high unemployment, which would receive both special funds under Section 6 and regular funds under Section 5. The Seattle area and Southern California (and other aerospace centers), depressed rural areas, and inner-city neighborhoods populated by low-income blacks and Spanish-speaking persons would benefit from this addition. Two or three small states gained by being assured of a minimum allocation under the Section 5 program. The combined effect was a gain for rural areas relative to urban areas.

The other congressional decision on distribution of benefits related to what share of program costs the national government would pay. Nelson's and Daniel's original bills provided that federal funds should not exceed 80 percent unless the secretary of labor waived this requirement in special local circumstances. States and localities would be expected to pay the remainder. The Senate committee reduced the nonfederal share to 10 percent, and the House committee eliminated it altogether. The conference committee accepted 10 percent but provided that this share could be provided in cash or kind; that is, state and local governments could furnish supplies, equipment, and personnel rather than put up cash. The effect of this decision was to shift more of the total cost to the federal tax system. The whole program, of course, would be beneficial to state and local governments, which could anticipate $2.25 billion dollars flowing their way for public-service activities during the next two years.

After Congress passed the Emergency Employment Act and President Nixon signed it, it was the administration's turn to act. On July 13, 1971, the day after he signed the bill, the President sent a request to Congress for an appropriation of $1 billion for the 1972 fiscal year, which had begun on July 1, 1971. This was the full amount authorized. In accordance with the act, it would be divided into three parts: $600 million, representing 80 percent of Section 5 funds, for the regular program, which had to be allocated by formula; $150 million consisting of the remaining funds from Section 5, which the secretary had discretion over; and $250 million for the special employment-assistance program authorized by Section 6. It took until January, 1972, for the administration to allocate the total fund, but the most controversial decisions were made in July in the allocation of $600 million of Section 5 funds according to formula.

The precise language of the act on allocation of Section 5 funds is this:

ambiguous

not less than 80 percentum shall be apportioned among the States in an equitable manner, taking into consideration the proportion which the total number of unemployed persons in each such State bears to such total number of such persons, respectively, in the United States.[7]

Labor Department technicians devised four alternative apportionment formulas. The first took the wording of the act literally and apportioned funds on the basis of the total number of unemployed in each state relative to the total number in the whole nation. The second formula focused upon severity of unemployment and apportioned funds on the basis of only the number of unemployed over 4.5 percent in each state, compared to the national total exceeding 4.5 percent. The third formula allocated half the funds by the first formula and half by the second so that both total number and severity were given consideration. The fourth formula used a more complicated system for weighing levels and rates of unemployment.

Departmental staff rejected the fourth formula as too complex to administer. They turned down the second formula because the eight states and the District of Columbia with unemployment rates less than 4.5 percent would receive only the $1.5 million minimum guaranteed each state by the statute, amounting to 2 percent of the funds, but these states, taken collectively, had 12 percent of the nation's unemployment. This left a choice between the first and third formulas. The planning technicians were inclined to favor the third one because it averaged out the differences resulting from considering either number or severity alone.

But this was a political decision, not one to be made by civil-service personnel. Therefore, first the political executives at the Labor Department (particularly Undersecretary Silberman and Assistant Secretary Lovell) gave the matter their attention, and then the issue moved to the Office of Management and Budget and the White House, where OMB Assistant Director Nathan and John Ehrlichman and the Domestic Council staff were involved. There severity factors, was preferable, and it was adopted. Secretary of was unanimity that the third formula, combining total number and

Labor Hodgson announced the state apportionment on July 23.

The decision favored twenty-three states and Puerto Rico where the unemployment rate was over 6.1 percent, for they were apportioned more funds than they would have received under a formula related only to number of unemployed. Conversely, twenty-seven states and the District of Columbia were apportioned less than they would have gained under the first formula. California would get $100 million under the formula chosen, 22.7 million more than under the rejected alternative. As Table I shows, other big gainers were Washington ($11.6 million) and Michigan ($10.4). Texas was the greatest loser ($10.3 million), followed by Illinois ($9.7 million).[8]

TABLE I

States Which Gained and Lost Most on EEA Formula Chosen
(*Alternative Three Compared to Alternative One*)*

Gainers		Losers	
State	Gain (in millions)	State	Loss (in millions)
California	$22.7	Texas	$10.3
Washington	11.6	Illinois	9.7
Michigan	10.4	Ohio	6.7
Puerto Rico	7.2	New York	6.4
New Jersey	4.9	Florida	6.2
Connecticut	4.8	Pennsylvania	6.2
Massachusetts	3.8	North Carolina	4.6
Oregon	2.0	Georgia	3.3
West Virginia	1.5 •	Maryland	3.2
Alaska	1.2	Virginia	3.0

*Methods of apportioning 80 percent of funds ($600 million) under Section 5 of Emergency Employment Act of 1971.

    Alternative 1 = Solely on basis of number unemployed.

    Alternative 3 = One-half on basis of total number unemployed, and one-half on basis of number of excess over 4.5 percent.

With state funds so apportioned, the Labor Department turned to local areas. The act stated that general local government was an eligible applicant for financial assistance, and theoretically this meant that 3,000 counties, 18,000 municipalities, and 17,000 townships might be eligible to apply. This was far too many to handle administratively, so the department invented the concept of "program agent" whereby a state or major local unit would receive, administer, and distribute funds to other eligible applicants. Cities with a population of at least 75,000 could be program agents, and so could counties with 75,000 or more residents living outside of eligible cities. State government would serve as program agent for the "balance-of-state."

Funds would be apportioned to local program agents on the same basis as to the states (that is, on the basis of a combination of amount and severity of unemployment). The states would have leeway in apportioning funds to localities under 75,000 in the balance-of-state, but they would be encouraged to take into consideration extent and severity of unemployment.

Congressional leaders and staff got wind of the department's plan to utilize program agents and expressed some concern about it. The previous year's manpower-reform legislation had provided for "prime sponsors" to work at the local level as the principal planning and coordinating body for comprehensive manpower programs. The administration's manpower-revenue-sharing bill had proposed 100,000 population as the minimum size for a prime sponsor, but Congress lowered that number to 75,000 because some of the committee members wanted to be sure that certain cities in their districts would be eligible. At first the Labor Department returned to the 100,000 figure in its tentative EEA guidelines, but it changed the figure to 75,000 after hearing from congressional staff who did not want a precedent established which would be hard to undo later in manpower-reform legislation. Even at this lower figure, some members of Congress opposed the program-agent concept.

They were even more upset by the apportionment formula to the states. In effect, what the Department of Labor had done was to adopt the concept of the Senate bill, which talked about both number and severity of unemployed, but which was dropped during conference because the special program of Section 6 was aimed at areas of very high unemployment. Once again, the department seemed to be going its own way and ignoring congressional intent.

Perkins wrote in protest and Daniels held a couple of informal hearings with Assistant Secretary Lovell to discuss the apportionment formula and the program-agent concept. Lovell argued that the act said the funds were to be "apportioned among the States in an equitable manner" and that equity required paying attention to severity of unemployment. Furthermore, he continued, the act said that "consideration" should be given to the number of unemployed, and this the department had done but without limiting apportionment to that factor alone. Program agents, he explained, were necessary to make the program manageable. Perkins and Daniels could argue with Lovell and make recommendations, but with the legislation already enacted they no longer had direct leverage on the department.

Congressional influence, though, could be exercised through the appropriations process, and this is where the dispute turned. Appropriations are handled by different committees than the ones which develop legislation authorizing programs. The appropriation committees of both houses of Congress work through subcommittees, and on July 28 a House subcommittee chaired by Daniel J. Flood of Pennsylvania held a hearing on the President's appropriations request of $1 billion. Lovell, representing the administration, brought with him a half-dozen staff members from the Labor Department. Flood raised questions about the formula, and so did Neal Smith of Iowa and George Mahon of Texas (Mahon was chairman of the full Appropriations Committee); all three were from states slated to receive less under the chosen formula. But in the end, the subcommittee did not attempt to alter the department's decisions.[9]

Members of the full House Appropriations Committee were more concerned about budget allocations. The Labor Department had budgeted $864 million for wages and participant benefits, $37 million for training and supportive services, and $99 million for federal, state, and local administration and technical assistance and statistics. The committee felt that the last item was excessive and accordingly allowed only $50 million, shifting $44 million more into wages and benefits and $5 million additional for training. With this change, the committee endorsed the $1-billion appropriation by a vote of 25 to 9.

After the appropriations bill had gone through the Rules Committee and reached the House floor on August 4, the battle about the formula was renewed. Representative Smith of Iowa offered an amendment to require that Section 5 funds be allocated solely upon number of unemployed. He was supported by Daniels, who stated that this had been legislative intent of the Labor Committee (though Daniels' home state of New Jersey would gain from the Labor Department's two-part formula). Quie and Steiger defended the administration. Smith's motion was voted down, 213 to 172. The other floor fight was on a motion by William D. Ford of Michigan to void the use of program agents, but his effort was defeated, 219 to 171. The Labor Committee leadership sided with Smith and Ford, but proponents of the motions did not organize support as thoroughly as was done when the basic legislation was before the House. Moreover, which states would benefit was not a party issue, so district interests became more of a factor.[10]

In the meantime, the Senate Appropriations Committee had also been considering the appropriations request, and a subcommittee chaired by Warren G. Magnuson of Washington conducted a hearing on July 27 at which Lovell and his associates appeared. The hearing was noncontroversial.[11] The full committee reported the appropriations resolution as soon as it was received from the House and made one policy directive stating that any employee laid off by an eligible applicant agency would have to wait thirty days before he or she could be rehired. On August 6 the Senate, at its last meeting before the summer recess, took up the appropriations resolution and adopted it.[12]

Thus, at the end of the appropriations process, the Labor Department's two-part formula for apportionment of Section 5 funds remained intact. However, Congress had shifted $49 million from administration to participant wages, leaving $50 million for project administration and $36 million earmarked for training and support activities. As a result, fully 91.4 percent of the budget would directly benefit the unemployed, compared to the 85 percent minimum in the authorizing legislation.

By this time, one further decision about beneficiaries had been made. In its guidelines, the Department of Labor set a goal that at least a third of all participants should be veterans. Except for this, program agents were required to select participants on an equitable basis from among all significant segments of the unemployed and underemployed population.

With the legislation passed, the appropriations made, and initial administrative regulations and guidelines adopted, the emergency-employment program was ready to roll into action.

PART TWO
ADMINISTRATIVE PHASE

5

FEDERAL
ADMINISTRATION

When the emergency-employment program entered the administrative phase, a new group of people and a different part of the federal administrative apparatus became involved. The role of Congress diminished and after a couple of months so did that of staff in the Executive Office of the President. Civil-service employees of the Department of Labor, topped by a handful of political executives, now became the dominant force in Washington and in ten regional offices around the country. Almost immediately state and local officials also became major actors.

Within the federal government, the Department of Labor undertook the administration of the Public Employment Program. Since gaining cabinet status in 1913, this department has always been the smallest of the federal executive departments (not counting independent agencies). However, during the 1960s the department personnel grew from 4,100 in 1961 to 11,300 in 1971. The expansion occurred mainly because of new manpower programs enacted during this decade, first the Manpower Development and Training Act of 1962, and then the Economic Opportunity Act of 1964, both subsequently amended several times to add new categorical programs.

Within the Labor Department, the Public Employment Program was assigned to the Manpower Administration, one of the department's five major program-operating units (the others are Labor-Management Services, Labor Statistics, Employment Standards, and Occupational Safety and Health). Since being established in

1963, the Manpower Administration has gone through almost yearly reorganization (as many federal agencies are always doing). It started as a merger, on paper, of two old-line bureaus and two new ones, and expanded from there as Congress enacted additional manpower programs until the internal structure became unwieldy. But attempts at administrative consolidation ran into conflicts among competing interests. The two long-established bureaucracies—the Bureau of Employment Security, which was allied with state employment-service agencies, and the Bureau of Apprenticeship and Training, which had close ties with the AFL-CIO—preferred to go their own ways. They would have little to do with the newer programs, which were run by the Office of Planning, Evaluation and Research and by the Bureau of Work and Training, whose constituency was community-action agencies and other new entrants in the manpower field.

Each bureau had its own regional arrangements, combining states differently and choosing as its regional headquarters whatever city suited its convenience. Each regional director reported to his bureau in Washington, and there was, therefore, relatively little regional coordination. In order to gain more control over the far-flung bureaucracy, Secretary of Labor Willard Wirtz issued an order in October, 1968, reorganizing the regional offices so that all the field units in each region would be under a regional manpower administrator, who would in turn be responsible to the manpower administrator in Washington. This would have severed the field units' direct ties to the specialized bureaus in Washington. But the state-employment-service lobby, adamantly against this change, mustered sufficient political pressure to get President Johnson to countermand the secretary's order.[1]

The following spring, Wirtz's successor, George Shultz, put into effect a similar plan except that the Bureau of Apprenticeship and Training kept its direct lines to the field. However, most of the regional manpower administrators and key positions in Washington were filled by employees with an employment-security background rather than with people from the newer programs, who would have had the jobs under Wirtz's plan. Under principles of the "new federalism" enunciated by President Nixon the regional manpower administrators were given wider decision-making authority, but there still remained in Washington offices and bureaus for all the major programs: Apprenticeship and Training, Unemployment Insurance, Employment Service, Job Corps, and Employment Development Programs.

This was the organizational scheme in effect when Congress passed the Emergency Employment Act of 1971. If the Executive Branch had been promoting this legislation, the Department of Labor would have had a task force planning the details of future program administration. Indeed, at that time both the Labor Department and the Department of Health, Education and Welfare had large task forces working on welfare reform. But since the White House was opposing emergency-employment legislation all winter and spring, most departmental personnel did nothing in this area. Exceptions to this were a few people in the Office of Planning, Evaluation and Research who wrote some speculative memoranda on such matters as the allocation formula, but these documents never reached the top policymakers.

When the President changed his mind in June, Undersecretary Silberman and Assistant Secretary Lovell were so busy working out compromise legislation that they had no time to think about administrative organization until after the House had voted approval of the conference committee report on July 1. When they began to consider how to run the new program, they had no doubt that field operations should be under the ten regional administrators. As to the Washington organization, the logic of past decisions suggested that responsibility should be assigned to the Office of Employment Development Programs, which was handling most of the programs initiated in the sixties. They conluded, however, that this large new program, in which the White House had suddenly acquired great interest, needed special attention and therefore a new and separate office. So, over the Independence Day weekend, they decided to create a new Office of Public Service Employment. On July 5 the position of director was offered to William Mirengoff, who was then director of the Job Corps. After mulling it over for a couple of days, he accepted.

Mirengoff was a career employee of the Department of Labor. In the 1950s he had served in the Bureau of Employment Security. He had been involved in the enactment of the Manpower Development and Training Act of 1962 and (for seven years) in planning and research operations funded by that act. He had taken charge of the Job Corps in the summer of 1969, when it was transferred to the Labor Department from the Office of Economic Opportunity.

In his new assignment, Mirengoff called upon persons with whom he had worked closely to join him. William Haltigan, who had been his deputy at the Job Corps, took a similar job in the Office of Public Service Employment. Albert J. Angebrandt, previously with the Job Corps and most recently with the Office of Occupational Safety and Health, rejoined Mirengoff and headed the Office of Program Policy, Planning and Procedures. Ludwin Branch was brought in from the Atlanta regional office and put in charge of the Office of Program Review and Agent Assistance. Mrs. Anna-Stina Ericson was transferred from the staff of the assistant secretary for planning, evaluation, and research to direct special program studies (earlier she had been with the Bureau of Labor Statistics). And most of the other jobs were filled by transferring personnel from other units of the Labor Department.

The Office of Public Service Employment was officially established on July 12, 1974, the day President Nixon signed the Emergency Employment Act. Rather than create a formal hierarchical structure immediately, Mirengoff chose to operate at the outset through a task-force approach. Among administrative theorists, this method is sometimes called "project management," also the "matrix model." The task force has no permanent boxes or lines of authority; instead, personnel are shifted about as one task is completed and the next one begun. Flexibility is the byword. In the case at hand, the Office of Public Service Employment operated in the task-force mode until the late fall of 1971.

The first tasks related to a series of policy decisions on fund allocation, on how to deal with states and localities, on guidelines, and on regulations.

The choices considered for allocation of Section 5 funds among the states have been discussed above, in chapter four. Mirengoff's staff worked on technical aspects of these matters, but presidential appointees in the Labor Department and the Executive Office of the President ultimately made the key decisions.

Regarding program administration, Labor Department personnel quickly decided that the Public Employment Program (PEP) —as they named it—should not be another categorical program, with thousands of individual grants or contracts from the federal government to local sponsors. Instead, it should have an administrative structure compatible with the kind of decentralized manpower-delivery system which they hoped Congress would soon be setting up in comprehensive manpower legislation. Essentially there were two choices.

One approach would be to have a Public Employment Program for each major labor-market area, utilizing the central city as prime sponsor and letting it contract with other units of government in the labor-market area. State government would perform a similar role in the balance-of-state. This had the advantage of an established data base for determining how much unemployment there was, and it was consistent with earlier legislative proposals of the administration. However, in most localities the necessary structural relationships between central cities and the remainder of the labor-market areas did not exist, and it would be hard to develop them rapidly for this program.

An alternative approach would be to designate large cities and counties as "agents" of the secretary of labor and to use the states in the same way in the remainder of the country. This would reduce the political problems of the labor-market approach and would eliminate the need for the department to deal with many small units of government. However, there were no adequate unemployment data by city and county to help guide fund allocation. Furthermore, foreclosing the use of labor-market areas would discourage the kind of interjurisdictional action which the department had been promoting.

In the end, the second choice presented fewer obstacles and was selected. As a population base, 50,000 was rejected as producing too many program agents, and 100,000, which was in the administration's manpower revenue-sharing bill, was opposed by congressional committees. This left 75,000 as the population base for program agents, and staff at OMB and in the White House ratified this figure.

Eleven days after President Nixon signed the Emergency Employment Act and the secretary of labor established the Office of Public Service Employment, Secretary Hodgson announced the allocation formula for $600 million of Section 5 funds and indicated that start-up funds, amounting to 20 percent of the allocation for each area, would go to state and local program agents as soon as Congress appropriated the money.[2] To make this administratively possible, the Office of Public Service Employment had four staff groups working feverishly on data, regulations and guidelines, grant procedures, and reporting instructions.

The Labor Department's information on local unemployment was only for whole labor-market areas, and it lacked the data on cities and counties necessary to allocate funds to program agents in jurisdictions of 100,000 or more. To fill the gap, the department turned to the state employment services, which have research and statistical sections with capability along these lines. They got this information to Washington during the first week in August, and by August 12, on the same day that the President signed the appropriations act, the secretary of labor was able to announce the allocation of funds within states.[3]

But before any money could be disbursed, the secretary had to adopt regulations and guidelines. Regulations are issued to set forth the department's construction of the act and to clear up any ambiguities in the legislation. They have the force of law and ordinarily must be published in the Federal Register forty-five days before taking effect. However, given the emergency nature of the program, notice of publication was determined to be impractical and the regulations went into effect on the day of publication, August 14.[4] Public comments were invited for forty-five days for consideration in later revisions.

Guidelines are more fully descriptive of how a program is to function, and in case of any discrepancy between guidelines and regulations, the regulations are controlling. The department issued its preliminary guidelines on the initial allocation of Section 5 funds on July 23 and a more complete revised version on August 27.

They covered such items as conditions for eligibility, allocation of funds, establishment of jobs, application and funding processes, training and supportive services, employee compensation and working conditions, records and reporting, financial procedures, and program terminations.[5]

The department made an early decision to disburse emergency-employment funds in the form of grants rather than contracts. Grants provide more flexibility for both the federal agency and the local recipient than do contracts, which include many more legal conditions. Material produced by the working group on grant procedures was incorporated into the guidelines, as were the reporting instructions developed by another work group.

As the department developed the regulations and guidelines, it conferred with major interest groups whose local constituents would be most heavily involved in program administration: the U. S. Conference of Mayors, the National League of Cities, the National Governors Conference, and the AFL-CIO and affiliated unions of public employees, teachers, and fire fighters. The department also asked the National Civil Service League to make recommendations on how local and state personnel systems could quickly hire unemployed persons.

In early August, as the appropriations bill moved through Congress, the Manpower Administration called its regional manpower administrators to Washington to explain the allocation formula for program agents and to go over the draft guidelines. Next, staff from the Office of Public Service Employment asked the regional offices to arrange meetings for Washington staff to make presentations to regional staff and representatives of prospective program agents.

The first grant was made on August 16, and the first PEP enrollee started work on the same day. By Labor Day almost all of the start-up grants had been approved and 3,000 participants had been employed. By then the Office of Public Service Employment, still operating in task-force fashion, had moved on to the subject of Section 6 funds, aimed at areas with unemployment of 6 percent or more. Allocation formulas and guidelines were drawn up and announced on September 20.[6] The regional manpower administrators came to Washington for another briefing, and staff from Office of

Public Service Employment went out once again to orient regional-office personnel. The same process was repeated for allocation of funds to Indian reservations, guidelines for which were issued on September 27.[7] A variation was used for the $150 millions in discretionary funds under Section 5, three-fourths of which went to a high impact demonstration program announced on October 8 (see chapter eleven).[8]

During the last three months of 1971 the Department of Labor had only small amounts of discretionary funds left in Section 5 and a small balance in Section 6 to allocate. But by then the major concern in Washington was pushing program agents to hire people more quickly, a pressure which came steadily from White House staff. This pressure was applied to cities, counties, and states by the department's regional offices, which handled review of grant applications and other direct contacts with program agents.

As noted previously, the department had budgeted $39 million for agent assistance and statistics, but this was knocked out by the House Appropriations Committee. The intention had been to use a variety of consultants to assist program agents. Instead, a much more modest technical-assistance effort was arranged in November. The Office of Public Service Employment worked out an agreement with the U. S. Civil Service Commission under which civil-service technicians in each region would help Labor Department regional offices and state and local program agents to devise methods for changing unnecessary personnel requirements and for transferring emergency employees to permanent career status. Another unit of the Manpower Administration entered into a contract with the National Association of Counties Research Foundation to conduct conferences and provide technical assistance to county manpower staffs on public employment and other manpower programs. Under another contract, the U. S. Conference of Mayors/National League of Cities was already engaged in similar activities. Later, the National Governors Conference also received a contract, but more to deal with comprehensive state manpower planning than with emergency employment.

By the early months of 1972 the Office of Public Service Employment had passed through its initial stage and was ready for a more stable structure to replace the continually changing task-force style. So the staff, totaling only sixty people, was divided into two divisions: an Office of Program, Policy, Planning and Procedures, and an Office of Program Review and Agent Assistance. Under the organizational scheme of the Manpower Administration, lines of communications with the regions went through the deputy manpower administrator. This was respected for formal communications, but there was also an informal arrangement whereby certain staff from the Office of Public Service Employment served as "regional desk officers," not as an exclusive assignment but in addition to other duties. Having commenced as a task force and being fairly small, this office never did become a highly structured operation.

At the beginning of 1972, the Office of Public Service Employment was dealing with 608 funded program agents. This number peaked at 657 in June, 1972, divided as follows:

	Number	Percent of $ Fiscal 1972
States and territories	55	28.2
Cities	239	40.8
Counties	368	30.1
Indian tribes and tribal organizations	23	.9
	685	100.0

How these program agents went about their tasks is the topic of the next three chapters.

6

CITY PROGRAMS

After the Department of Labor had made its decisions on allocations and program agents and promulgated regulations and guidelines, it was ready to grant emergency-employment funds to the states and to cities and counties of over 75,000 in population. As this occurred, new sets of political and administrative relationships arose between different levels of the federal system, between agencies within state and local government, and between the program agents and other jurisdictions, which became "subagents" and "employing agents." Around the country, the program took different configurations. This chapter examines what emerged in cities. The following chapter looks at county, substate-district, and Indian programs, and the chapter after that reviews the role of state government.[1]

Getting Organized

Historically, cities are newcomers to the manpower field. Although they were involved in New Deal emergency-work programs, most of those programs were temporary, and only the state employment services, created in 1934, came out of the thirties with permanent status. When the Manpower Training and Development Act of 1962 became law, the employment services and the state vocational-education systems gained primacy. Under the Economic Opportunity Act of 1964, community-action agencies, most of which were private nonprofit organizations, joined the manpower field. Two local efforts of manpower coordination began in 1967. The Cooperative Area Manpower Planning Systems (CAMPS) brought together local agency representatives in an advisory committee, at first chaired and staffed by employment-services personnel. And the Concentrated Employment Program (CEP), aimed at disadvantaged persons in sixty-six designated inner-city neighborhoods and fourteen rural areas, usually had community-action agencies as prime sponsors and state employment services as the prime deliverers of service.

The first serious effort to involve city government came in 1968, when the Labor Department gave central-city mayors the chance to chair or appoint the chairmen of the local CAMPS committees. Two years later, the department offered funds to mayors of the 130 largest cities to hire manpower-planning staff. And starting in 1969, a program called Public Service Careers (PSC) gave cities money to hire disadvantaged persons and then train them for civil-service jobs (locally this was usually handled by the personnel department or civil-service commission). Thus, by the summer of 1971, when the Public Employment Program got underway, almost every city of over 100,000 people had at least a skeletal manpower staff (and a number of them had considerably more than that).

For the emergency-employment program, each city could organize in its own way. Forty-five percent of the cities assigned this program to the personnel department, 21 percent to the manpower-planning unit, 17 percent to the office of mayor or city manager, and the other 17 percent to departments of human resources, planning, budget, or finance.[2] Mayor-council cities tended to operate differently than council-manager cities.

Six cities can serve as illustrations, starting with how they organized to apply for and use the basic program funds under Section 5 of the Emergency Employment Act.

New York (population 7,900,000) is one of the few cities which has a major city department for manpower, the Manpower and Career Development Agency, which was established in 1966 as a part of the city's supersize Human Resources Administration (HRA). In July, 1971, however, Mayor John V. Lindsay set up a separate, seven-member EEA Policy Committee to decide how to spend the city's $15.8 million in emergency-employment Section

5 funds. The committee consisted of the administrator of HRA, the budget director, the director of personnel, the model-cities administrator, the chairman of the Commission on Human Rights, the first assistant to the corporate counsel, and the head of the Department of Labor Relations. The first three took on primary responsibility for implementing the program. The Human Resources Administration undertook basic administration, at first dividing the tasks among existing units but later creating a special PEP unit. The Budget Bureau added staff to its office of federal and state programs to determine appropriate assignment of job "slots" to different agencies. The Department of Personnel took on the task of hiring.[3]

In *Chicago* (population 3,400,000), Mayor Richard C. Daley, whose executive powers are enhanced by his position as political-party leader, had established in 1970 a Mayor's Office for Manpower and designated the head of this office to be chairman of the CAMPS committee. By the summer of 1971 this office had conducted contingency planning for public-service employment, the Civil Service Commission had recently assessed the manpower needs of the civil-service system, and the city had implemented a Public Service Careers Program. Working together, the Mayor's Office for Manpower and the Personnel Department in the Civil Service Commission took on responsibility for getting PEP funded and underway. When departmental requests for jobs far exceeded the $7.8 million allotted Chicago under Section 5, the mayor appointed a five-member steering committee, composed of his top administrative assistant, his assistant for manpower, the director of personnel, the budget officer, and the comptroller, to determine priorities.[4]

In *Milwaukee* (population 717,000), the Common Council, with the mayor's approval, established in 1966 the Intergovernmental Fiscal Liaison Department for the purpose of seeking additional financial assistance from state and federal agencies. In 1971 it was this department that took on the task of getting the $3 million in EEA Section 5 funds that were earmarked for Milwaukee. But to administer the program, Mayor Henry Maier designated the Civil Service Commission, which was already handling Public Service Careers and several other special manpower programs in addition to conventional personnel responsibilities.[5]

In a council-manager city such as *San Diego* (population 697,000) the mayor's role is limited mainly to presiding over the city council and serving as ceremonial head of the city. Breaking with this tradition, the incumbent mayor in 1965 set up the Mayor's Committee on Jobs to deal with unemployment problems, and in 1970 the mayor assumed chairmanship of the CAMPS committee and appointed two staff assistants. The mayor's acquisition of staff was viewed dubiously by the city manager, who by charter and custom is administrative head of all city operations, and when the Public Employment Program came along, the manager's office took charge. An assistant city manager and staff from the Personnel Department, which is under the Civil Service Commission, prepared the application for the $1.9 million of Section 5 funds. Toward the end of 1971, a new Human Resources Department was established under the manager, and it took over PEP, the model-cities program, and staff works for CAMPS. The mayor, a different person by then, remained chairman of CAMPS.[6]

Winston-Salem (population 132,000), also with a council-manager government, is a manufacturing city in the Piedmont region of North Carolina. It has a fairly cohesive economic and political power structure, business dominated but providing a place for black leaders. The same "governing coalition" controls both the city and surrounding Forsyth County, and this leadership group decided to combine the $400,000 in Section 5 funds allocated to the city and the $48,000 allotted the county into a single program run by the city. Responsibility for developing the program was assigned to the director of the Concentrated Employment Program (CEP), who was on the city payroll, and later, when he was promoted to assistant city manager, he combined responsibility for emergency employment, CEP, and the mayor's manpower-planning grant.[7]

The Public Employment Program in *Decatur, Illinois* (population 90,000) was placed under the city manager. Since the incumbent manager was leaving to take a position in another city just as PEP was starting, one of his assistants took charge and prepared the application for the city's $113,000 under Section 5.[8]

Getting Funded and Assigning Positions

As indicated in chapter four, the Labor Department decided to quickly give program agents 20 percent of their anticipated allocation, and to this end, during the second week of August, 1971, regional staff of the Manpower Administration got in touch with cities to tell them how much they could expect in initial funding. Moreover, the regional staff set a ten-day deadline—and sooner if possible—for getting the applications in and promised rapid approval so that unemployed persons could be hired by the end of the month. This amazed municipal officials, who were used to months of waiting for federal-application review.

The guidelines required that the application for initial funding describe the jobs to be filled, the departments and other governmental units which would serve as subgrantees, and the costs. Within another thirty days, the application for full funding would be required, describing more fully the area to be covered, the population served, the public-service needs, and the methods for distributing jobs and funds among other jurisdictions within the program agent's area. This meant that cities had immediately to assign PEP jobs to various agencies.

The task of deciding how to use the PEP money in *New York* was handled primarily by the city's Bureau of the Budget, which knew where personnel needs were greatest because of a job freeze it was administering. Therefore, the budget director, an official quite close to the mayor, selected the agencies and types of jobs for initial funding, weighing both service needs and the impact of recent budget cuts. For full funding, the EEA Policy Committee was more fully involved, but individual agencies were given considerable discretion in deciding how to assign their allocated positions. The Board of Education, which is financially part of the city government, got nearly a third of the positions, the Health and Hospitals Administration was next, and the Police Department third.

In *Chicago*, the Mayor's Office for Manpower and the Personnel Department worked together to prepare the application, the latter identifying the jobs to be filled and the former developing the budget and other details. At this point, the city decided to bring in the

Board of Education and the Park District, two independent taxing jurisdictions, as subagents and to allocate sums to them. Education got the most positions, followed by streets and sanitation and then police.

Shortly after the President signed the Emergency Employment Act, *Milwaukee's* Civil Service Commission surveyed city departments to determine how they might best use EEA funds, particularly for projects for which city funds had been previously requested but denied. As it worked out, public works got the most positions, followed by city development and the school board. The Intergovernmental Fiscal Liaison Department put the application together, but before it could be submitted, the city's Common Council had to approve (reflecting its larger role in governance than its counterparts in New York and Chicago). Since the council was in its August recess, the city clerk conducted a telephone poll and gained unanimous approval.

In preparing the *San Diego* application, the Office of City Manager asked city departments and the San Diego Unified School District (an independent body) to list the number of jobs required to catch up on existing programs and to provide needed new services. The response was overwhelming, and the total number of proposed jobs far exceeded available resources. The school district alone asked for enough jobs to use up all the funds. Intensive negotiations ensued, and in the end the school district received a third of the jobs. As for the rest, the assistant city manager and the Personnel Department worked out assignments to city departments, giving priority to jobs with high turnover (which would ease transition into permanent jobs) and to critical maintenance or renovation activities. Then the application went to the City Council for its approval.

In preparing the *Winston-Salem* application, the program director was able to utilize staff from the Concentrated Employment Program, which he had been running, to call on the mayor's manpower-planning staff, which had been working on CAMPS, and to borrow an employee from the Labor Department's regional office in Atlanta under the Intergovernmental Personnel Act. The director called together representatives of city and county agencies and asked them to propose positions, and from these "want" lists the staff selected jobs, giving heavy emphasis to jobs which could be filled by disadvantaged blacks. They assigned positions to city and county agencies, the Board of Education, and the public hospital.

In *Decatur*, the city manager's assistant held a meeting with city department heads and another meeting with other potential sub-agents, inviting them to submit proposals for funding. From their submissions, he developed a list suggesting the most beneficial mix of positions, based upon severity of public-service needs and potential composition of the work force. This list went to the City Council, which made the decisions on what agencies to use and what jobs to fill. Decatur's Section 5 funds produced seven city jobs, five with the school district, and two each with the sanitary and park districts.

The regional offices of the Labor Department immediately approved all the applications for initial funding. Some of the proposals for full funding took a little negotiation, but compared to the usual federal-grant process, action was swift. All concerned wanted the unemployed hired as soon as possible.

Recruitment and Hiring

Federal regulations and guidelines spelled out who would be eligible to participate in the program, mainly elaborating upon the basic act but allowing considerable flexibility in the recruitment and selection processes. The regulations required program agents to list all job vacancies (except former employees being recalled) with the state employment service, which would have forty-eight hours priority in which to recruit and refer eligible veterans. Other agencies concerned with job placement of veterans would be accorded similar priority.

In a number of places the hiring process raised issues involving the civil-service system and the municipal unions which had to be resolved before the program could move ahead. And in some places city government and the Labor Department disagreed as to when laid-off employees could be recalled.

Union power, reinforced by civil-service regulations, was a particularly significant factor in *New York*. The EEA Policy Committee, influenced by the United Federation of Teachers and other municipal unions, decided that about a fourth of the positions should be used to rehire laid-off employees, most of them teachers. To prevent the hiring of unemployed persons for middle-level civil-service jobs, which might be filled through promotion from within, the unions insisted that most of the other positions be for entry-level jobs. By civil-service requirements, these would have to be provisional appointments for persons who could qualify for permanent civil-service status, and therefore the EEA job descriptions were close to existing civil-service positions. The result was that many persons from disadvantaged backgrounds, including veterans, could not qualify. Another result of New York's decisions on which jobs to fill was a bimodal salary distribution, with the majority of laid-off employees returning to $10,000 to $12,000 jobs, and most provisional appointees filling $5,000 to $7,000 jobs at the bottom of the municipal pay scale.

Neither municipal unions nor civil-service regulations were as strong in *Chicago,* where Mayor Daley has habitually dealt with unions on an informal basis rather than through collective bargaining, and where a sizable number of city jobs have long been part of a political-patronage system. Newspaper publicity about the program produced many inquiries about jobs even before the application was filed with the Labor Department, and as soon as it was approved the Civil Service Commission reassigned twenty staff members to handle applicant interviewing and screening. The Board of Education took care of its own recruitment, recalling former teacher aides for some jobs and working with Latin American organizations to find bilingual teacher aides. The Park District also did its own hiring. The State Employment Service produced relatively few applicants, and most of these were low-skilled welfare recipients who qualified only for low-ranking positions—jobs filled first from the city's own file.

Milwaukee has nineteen separate municipal unions, but they adopted a cooperative approach to the Public Employment Program. Their main concern was rehiring procedures. Once funds were secured, the Mayor's Office and the Intergovernmental Fiscal Liaison Department got out of the act and let the Civil Service Commission handle the hiring. Six persons applied for every vacancy. Veterans were given highest priority, laid-off city employees were second, and graduates of federal manpower programs and disadvantaged applicants turned down for oversubscribed training programs were third. In contrast to the situation in New York, formal-education requirements were not a great roadblock to hiring disadvantaged persons under civil service in Milwaukee.

Civil service in *San Diego* operates under the "rule of three." That is, for each job opening the top three names on an eligibility list are certified to the department. In order for PEP to operate within the civil-service system, the city developed a hiring-hall technique. Representatives of several departments with similar personnel needs would assemble in one large room and interview a number of people who had been certified by the Civil Service Commission as eligible for emergency employment. These persons went to the different departmental desks to find out what jobs were available. At the end of the interview period, the applicants and the departments recorded their preferences, and then civil-service personnel matched persons and jobs. Later, though, the City Council amended the civil-service rules to permit selective certification of persons eligible for PEP jobs.

Having neither a civil-service system nor municipal unions, *Winston-Salem* had a freer hand in recruiting people for PEP jobs. The recruitment networks of the Concentrated Employment Program, which reached into black neighborhoods, was used primarily, but the State Employment Security Commission was also involved. Hiring was handled by the city, the county, the school board, and the hospital according to their usual procedures, and was the responsibility of the city manager in the case of the city itself.

In *Decatur*, the Illinois State Employment Service referred prospective employees to the subagents, who did their own hiring. For a while, the city was involved in a dispute with the municipal-employees union, which feared that emergency-employment funds would be used to fill civil-service jobs currently being eliminated, but the union was reassured on this point and the dispute was settled amicably. Although PEP participants were not made part of the regular civil-service system, they were given preference points toward future city jobs and were permitted to join the union.

Section 6

By the time the cities had submitted applications for full funding under Section 5, the Department of Labor had issued its guidelines for Section 6, the special-employment program aimed at areas with unemployment above 6 percent. This occurred on September 20, and the department gave the cities until October 6 to submit applications. Since the program agents would be the same, for cities this meant, for the most part, a repetition of the processes utilized for the Section 5 application.

There was a significant difference, however. Persons being hired had to come from the areas of high unemployment, and in the cities these were the poverty neighborhoods. The guidelines also specified that, wherever possible, jobs should also be located in such areas and that the public services rendered should benefit the residents, though jobs located within a reasonable commuting distance might also be considered.

In *New York*, the twenty-six poverty areas designated for the Community Action Program were used for the $7.7 million in Section 6 funds but were now grouped into seven areas. Once again the Bureau of the Budget determined which agencies would be allocated funds for what jobs. This time the Health and Hospitals Administration got the most jobs, nearly a fourth of the total, mostly for nonprofessional aides. The Board of Education was second, primarily for social-service aides rather than rehired teachers. Indeed, most of New York's Section 6 jobs were for entry-level civil-service positions.

The $3.4 million of Section 6 funds in *Chicago* went to twenty-six distinct areas of high unemployment, which had been identified by a special manpower-planning committee prior to enactment of the Emergency Employment Act. The Labor Department not only accepted these areas but indicated the amount of money assigned to each. However, to the chagrin of Chicago officials, the department's allocations were not proportional to the amount or rate of unemployment in these areas, and dividing the funds so many ways made administration more complicated. The Personnel Department simplified the task by asking each agency to indicate the job sites of unfilled positions from the Section 5 program, and those within the eligible areas were used for Section 6 hiring.

Milwaukee outlined an Economic Development Impact Area for its $735,000 in Section 6 projects, encompassing about a third of the city and including the model-cities area and the district served previously by the Concentrated Employment Program. The Civil Service Commission asked the agencies to come up with projects and jobs which could be filled by disadvantaged persons from the area, and as a result, most of the positions were for laborers and nonprofessional aides.

Unemployment in the *San Diego* area as a whole exceeded 6 percent. Nevertheless, federal regulations required that city's $633,000 in Section 6 funds be used to hire unemployed persons in identifiable pockets with appreciably higher rates of unemployment. But except for this restriction, Section 6 funds blended into the City of San Diego's regular program.

In *Winston-Salem*, the Section 6 area was the Concentrated Employment Program area. Since CEP formed the nucleus for recruitment for PEP, there was no perceptible difference in the process used to fill Section 5 jobs.

An inner-city area of *Dectaur* was given enough Section 6 money for six jobs, of which three went to the city, one to the school district, and two to the housing authority. Hiring followed the same process as the Section 5 program.

City Council

The role of city councils in getting the emergency-employment program underway varied with the form of municipal government. In the two largest of the cities discussed, New York and Chicago, the mayor had sufficient authority to negotiate federal grants and to enter into contracts without obtaining council approval. In Milwaukee, the Common Council is stronger relative to the mayor and had to approve the application. In all three council-manager cities

(San Diego, Winston-Salem, and Decatur) approval by council was required before an application could be submitted.

National League of Cities/U. S. Conference of Mayors

Before the National League of Cities and the U. S. Conference of Mayors merged some of their operations in 1970 the latter had a contract with the Labor Department to hold seminars for mayors and their staffs so that they could be better informed about federal manpower programs. This effort was folded into the merger and soon became a permanent feature, with continuing federal contracts of over $400,000 a year. When the Labor Department began giving manpower-planning grants to mayors in 1970, NLC/USCM ran seminars for them, and when the Public Employment Program came along, it was added to the agenda. At conferences for city manpower planners held at various locations around the country in October, 1971, and in January, May, and October, 1972, emergency employment was a primary focus of attention.

During the organizational days following passage of the Emergency Employment Act, NLC/USCM manpower staff met frequently with Labor Department personnel to discuss draft regulations and guidelines. As they learned of new policy decisions, they shared this information with city manpower directors. In addition, NLC/USCM received funds to conduct studies on different aspects of the Public Employment Program, including involvement of significant segments of the community, transition to permanent jobs, and public-service impact in terms of new and improved services. Information was obtained by a questionnaire sent to every city acting as program agent, by case studies in several locales, and by small seminars with a dozen or so local manpower directors to discuss key issues.[9]

Within the joint operations of the National League of Cities/ U. S. Conference of Mayors, one group of staff gave attention to legislation and functioned as lobbyists, while another group dealt with the federal department on policy issues, provided information to mayors and their staffs, and conducted research.

7

COUNTY, SUBSTATE-DISTRICT, AND INDIAN PROGRAMS

Many counties were entitled to become program agents for emergency employment. According to Labor Department regulations, eligible counties included those with 75,000 inhabitants living outside any city of 75,000. Altogether, 368 out of 3,064 counties became active program agents.

For the remaining counties, governors would serve as program agents but could choose to utilize counties as subagents. Another option for rural areas without city or county program agents would be to rely upon multicounty bodies, such as councils of government or regional planning districts, for the subagent role. Indian reservations were an exception, for they were covered by separate provisions.

In the following discussion, the experience of four counties, two substate districts, and two Indian programs will serve to illustrate how PEP operated outside cities.

Getting Organized and Assigning Positions

The most common form of county government has a commission of three to five members who collectively serve as the county's legislative body, and who also act as administrators, either as a body or as individual "commissioners." (In some states, the title is "supervisor" or "county judge.") Quite a few larger counties have added a full time manager or chief administrative officer to this system. And an increasing number of counties in metropolitan areas

82

have switched to the county executive-council form, with administrative and legislative powers divided between an elected chief executive, who functions like a "mayor" (though he is not called that), and the county council. Most counties have had less experience with manpower programs than cities, but in almost half of the states counties handle public assistance, which in recent years has developed employment activities.

In *San Diego County* (population 1,400,000), the five-member Board of Supervisors appoints a chief administrative officer who directs the work of eight major administrative agencies. One of these, the Human Resources Agency, was designated to prepare the application for the county's $1.7 million in Section 5 funds and to administer the Public Employment Program. The county decided to share this money with other governmental units outside the City of San Diego. A flat allocation was made to an intertribal council of Indians, and the rest was divided as follows: one-third to the twelve cities (ranging in population from 3,400 to 68,000), one-third to the forty-four school districts, and one-third to county agencies. County officials met with school superintendents, city managers, and other city officials to explain the program guidelines. For jobs within county government, the director of the Human Resources Agency and the chief administrative officer worked together to canvas the agencies and assign jobs on the basis of need for additional personnel.[1]

Champaign County, Illinois (population 162,000) contains the twin cities of Champaign (population 56,000) and Urbana (population 33,000) and the city of Rantoul (population 25,000). The chairman of the Board of Supervisors was designated official program agent, but he delegated administrative responsibility to the Champaign County Regional Planning Commission. In order to prepare the application, the commission sent a questionnaire on public-service employment needs to the principal county agencies and the three cities. Although the county was allocated $125,000 in Section 5 funds, the Labor Department's regulations provided that this would be divided between local and state government in proportion to the number of public jobs in the county. Because of the presence of the main campus of University of Illinois in Urbana, 70 percent of all public employment in the county is state employment, which meant that the county itself had only $35,000 to spend. When the county agencies and cities turned in a list of jobs which would require twelve times this amount to finance, the planning commission set up a council of agency representatives to help determine priorities. Preference was given to agencies serving the entire county rather than individual communities and to the public services of greatest need. In the end, the eight available positions were assigned to three county agencies: the Nursing Home, the Probation Department, and the Sheriff's Department.[2]

Robeson County (population 85,000), located in the southeastern coastal plain of North Carolina, was allocated $253,000 in Section 5 funds. The Board of County Commissioners assigned the county manager responsibility for preparing an application. He solicited assistance from the regional council of governments and the state's Employment Security Commission. By telephone and in a hastily called meeting, he conferred with potential employing agents and obtained proposals from six towns, six school districts, the local community college, a mental health center, and two special-purpose agencies, as well as from regular county agencies. Most of these jurisdictions were assigned positions, primarily for low-skill jobs: janitorial workers, grounds keepers, garbage collectors, street cleaners, school watchmen, general office clerks, a cook, and several aides. Only three jobs approached professional status, a caseworker for the regional mental health clinic, a public-health officer for the county, and a city-planning aide for Lumberton, the county's largest city (population 17,000).[3]

Bell County, in the eastern part of Kentucky, has only 31,000 residents and thus did not qualify as a program agent. Instead, it served as a subagent of the state, starting with a Section 5 subgrant of $122,000. Within state government, a newly established Emergency Employment Office handled the program, and it utilized multicounty area-development districts to reach out to the counties and provide them with technical assistance in preparing their application. In Bell County, the county judge, who is the chief elected officer, was named program subagent. He worked with the two supervisors, who serve with him on the county governing body and with the county superintendent of schools to identify jobs and to select priorities for work. They divided the jobs among the county, the school system, the cities of Middlesboro (population 12,000) and Pineville (population 3,000), and several state and private nonprofit agencies. The county used five of its positions to hire unemployed persons as PEP administrative staff. Most of the other jobs required fairly low skills, but there was work for a juvenile-program coordinator, a social worker, and a plumber-electrician.[4]

In Texas, only 14 of the 254 counties were eligible to become program agents on their own. To fulfill his balance-of-state obligations in the other 240, the governor turned to the twenty-four councils of government, which are voluntary, multicounty bodies covering most of the state. One of these, the *South Texas Development Council (STDC),* is composed of four counties (Jim Hogg, Starr, Webb, Zapata) and the city of Laredo, all represented on its board of directors. The combined population is 100,000 people. As the state had done for balance-of-state allocations, so STDC used the Labor Department's two-part formula (number and severity of unemployment) to divide its $588,000 in Section 5 funds among the four counties. The City of Laredo and the four counties determined what jobs would be created with their assigned funds. They ranged from laborers to police officers, an assistant librarian, and a waterworks operator.[5]

In Massachusetts counties are quite limited functionally, and few of them reflect natural population groupings. So the state's Office of Manpower Affairs, in fulfilling the governor's program-agent responsibilities, utilized consortia of towns as subagents. The first one organized was in the westernmost portion of the state, and although it encompasses all of Berkshire County (population 149,000), it is not a county agency. Rather it is organized as the *Berkshire Manpower Commission,* which has representatives of all the towns with voting power proportionate to population. The mayor of Pittsfield, the largest city (population 57,000), becan. chairman and the mayor of North Adams (population 19,000), second in size, was chosen vice-chairman. The commission hired a staff director who prepared an application for the $559,000 available in Section 5 funds. He was able to draw upon previous studies made by the area's CAMPS committee, which had set the stage for organizing the consortium. The Commission decided to concentrate its attention on the disadvantaged and so chose jobs not requiring high levels of skill. These were assigned to cities, towns, and private nonprofit organizations, which used them for a wide variety of jobs, particularly jobs new to the area, such as day care, youth services, regional planning, and others.[6]

Another kind of consortium was used for Indians. In guidelines released on September 27, 1971, the Department of Labor announced that Indian program agents might consist of (a) tribes or combinations of tribes with 75,000 or more in population, (b) regional tribal organizations or multistate combinations of tribes, (c) statewide tribal organizations, or (d) the largest tribe in a state, if there were no regional or statewide tribal organization. Under these provisions, the *Montana Intertribal Policy Board* became the program agent for the seven Indian tribes in Montana which make up its membership. The combined reservation population in Montana is 24,000. The Labor Department, for its own administrative convenience, added the Wind River Reservation (population 4,400), the only one in Wyoming, but as the program developed the Joint Business Council of the two tribes there, the Shoshone and the Arapahoe, objected to being included.

Since the Montana Intertribal Policy Board is essentially an advisory and consultative body and lacks a permanent staff or offices, it contracted with Tri-State Tribes, Inc. to handle administrative details. This organization, based at the University of Montana in Billings and having representation from tribes in Montana, Wyoming, and Idaho, had been organized earlier as a technical-assistance and training organization under the community-action program. It proceeded to develop the application for the $706,000 in PEP funds allocated to the Montana tribes and the Wind River Reservation. The Labor Department had already allocated a sum to each tribe, so the main task was to work out the positions of the 136 jobs. The largest number were for parks and recreation, public-works jobs came second, and law enforcement third, but each tribe had its own priorities.[7]

In several cases a single tribe became a program agent. This was true for the *Navajo Nation*, the largest reservation in both geographic area and, with 150,000 inhabitants, in population. The Navajos, with their considerable economic resources and able leadership, are moving toward substantial independence from the Bureau of Indian Affairs and are taking over many functions previously administered by it. To participate as a manpower planning area in the CAMPS system, the Navajo Nation had established an Office of Manpower Planning under the tribal chairman, who is the elected chief executive. This office was therefore in a position to plan expeditiously for the use of the $3 million in PEP funds allocated to the Navajos. Departments of tribal government and two service subsidiaries, the Office of Navajo Economic Opportunity and the Tribal Housing Authority, were asked to identify jobs, and they came up with six times as many as the available funds would finance. The Office of Manpower Planning made assignments based upon proration of jobs requested and assessment of departmental capacity to absorb extra operating costs. When the program went into operation, it was placed in a new unit under the head of the Administrative Division, who also had responsibility for the Personnel Office.[8]

Recruitment and Hiring

These various county, district, and Indian programs moved rapidly to fill the emergency-employment jobs. *San Diego County,* in contrast to the City of San Diego, decided to bypass the regular civil-service system and set up a parallel operation. No civil-service examinations were required, which meant faster hiring but less assurance of later placement in permanent jobs. The cities and school districts handled their own recruitment and hiring.

The eight emergency-employment positions controlled by *Champaign County* were soon filled, and when, after a few months, three persons resigned, replacements were quickly found. Most of the applicants were referred by the State Employment Service, and each participating agency made its own hiring decisions.

Robeson County, with forty-nine jobs under Section 5 funds, had previously participated in a multicounty, rural version of the

Concentrated Employment Program and accordingly had experience in reaching out to the unemployed. This recruitment network was administered by the North Carolina Employment Security Commission, which assumed responsibility for referring people to the emergency-employment jobs. The veterans' contact man at the commission was particularly aggressive, and nearly half of the jobs were filled by veterans.

Recruitment in *Bell County* was handled by the Kentucky Employment Security Department through a branch office in Middlesboro, where one person was assigned two days a week to this task. First priority was given to veterans and second to disadvantaged persons. The recruiter searched the department's files and notified the Veterans Administration, the American Legion, the school systems, the community action agency, and the public-assistance and food-stamp offices that the jobs were available. For each position, three persons were referred to the official in charge of selection. The county judge made hiring decisions for county jobs, but he conferred with the superintendent of schools before choosing persons to work in the school system. Since the county has no civil-service system, he had flexibility, and comparative need for employment was a major factor in his determinations.

For the program run through the *South Texas Development Council*, the Texas Employment Commission took on primary responsibility for recruiting and certifying eligible persons. These were referred to the four counties and to the City of Laredo, which made their own hiring decisions. The counties do not have civil-service requirements. Laredo does, but most of the jobs were put outside the civil-service system. When the city tried to add four policemen and four firemen positions under civil service with PEP funds, complications arose and the money was reprogrammed to non-civil-service jobs.

Wage levels were another issue that arose in South Texas. Laredo and three counties paid some PEP workers the federal minimum of $1.60, as required, while regular workers in the same types of jobs continued to receive less. When the Labor Department's regional office in Dallas became aware of the situation, in November, 1971, it ruled that this practice violated regulations and that all PEP jobs had to be for occupations in which the pre-vailing rate was $1.60 or more. STDC contested the department's ruling on the ground that the regular jobs met the Texas minimum wage of $1.40 an hour. Furthermore, STDC saw the differential as a wedge to raise the local wage structure. After considerable paper work and long discussions, the regional office granted a waiver and allowed the jobs to be utilized.

The *Berkshire Manpower Commission* gave early attention to the recruitment process in order to assure that jobs were open to all and to bypass problems of "creaming" and political patronage. Therefore, the commission set up a system of eligibility certification and designated the local offices of the Neighborhood Youth Corps, the Work Incentive Program, the Community Action Program, the Department of Employment Security, and the Environmental Center of Berkshire Community College as certifying agencies. Then the commission developed a priority system for ranking applicants, as follows: (1) Indochina and Korean veterans (for the first two days of an opening), (2) primary wage earner unemployed for six months or longer and family income below poverty level (for the next two weeks), (3) primary wage earner of a poor family unemployed three months or longer (for two more weeks), and (4) primary wage earner seeking employment for four weeks or more (only after thirty days). Within each category, preference was given to younger and older persons, migrant farm workers, and non-English-speaking persons. Certified applicants were referred to the employing agents, which interviewed them and decided whether to hire; if they did not, they had to justify such action to the commission.

The *Montana Intertribal Policy Board* was not directly involved in recruitment because this was handled by each tribe individually. Typically the tribal PEP staff would post notices of available jobs and perhaps place an ad in the tribal newspaper, and a screening committee would make the selection. The state employment-service offices in Montana and Wyoming had little involvement. Employment-assistance offices run by the Bureau of Indian Affairs partici-pated to some extent but were not a major factor.

The *Navajo* reservation is divided into five administrative jurisdictions, called "agencies" by the Bureau of Indian Affairs. At each agency office, a PEP counselor and job developer handled recruitment, interviewing, and placement in PEP jobs. They received some assistance from BIA employment assistants and outreach offices of the state employment service, but mostly the tribal staff took care of the recruitment process.

Section 6

Of the county, district, and Indian programs here considered, all received funds under Section 6 except for Champaign County, where countywide unemployment was less than 6 percent and there was no identifiable pocket of high unemployment. The counties of San Diego and Robeson, acting as program agents, received their Section 6 allocations directly from the Labor Department. Bell County, Kentucky, and three counties in South Texas (Starr, Webb, and Zapata) were listed in the department's allocation under balance-of-state and got Section 6 funds as subagents, and the Commonwealth of Massachusetts allocated Section 6 money to the Berkshire Manpower Commission from the balance-of-state fund. Although Jim Hogg County, Texas, had a high unemployment rate, it has so few people that its allocation would have been under $25,000 and the department did not make allocations that small.

By and large, there was no greater difference in how Section 5 and Section 6 funds were handled in these county and district programs since entire counties qualified rather than specific areas. One additional grant went to Webb County in South Texas for a special migrant worker project under discretionary Section 5 funds; it had restrictions on type of participants but the jobs were mostly the same.

For the Indian programs, Section 5 and Section 6 funds were lumped together in the original grant so that there was never a distinction between the two sources in the grants made to the Montana Intertribal Policy Board and to the Navajo Nation.

National Association of Counties

In November, 1971, the Manpower Administration's Office of

Planning, Evaluation and Research made a $118,000 grant to the National Association of Counties Research Foundation to help build the capacity of counties in planning and implementing the manpower programs. Much of the effort of the County Manpower Project focused on the Public Employment Program because PEP represented the entrance of most counties into the manpower field.

The County Manpower Project held seven one-day workshops in different regional-headquarters cities, and emergency employment was a major topic of concern. It was a subject covered repeatedly in the bimonthly *County Manpower Report* and in articles in NACO's weekly *County News*. In December, 1971, NACO organized an EEA Task Force, which has met periodically to develop recommendations on administrative and program improvements needed as seen from the county perspective.[9]

From this base, the County Manpower Project developed a proposal to expand the role of counties in manpower planning. It requested the Labor Department to designate large counties as official manpower area planning bodies with staff paid by federal funds. The case was based upon the counties' experience running PEP and the fact that in three-fourths of these 104 counties no city had manpower-planning funds from the Labor Department. In August, 1973, the department announced that 154 counties with 150,000 or more residents outside the central city could receive a manpower planning grant. What this meant was that, as a byproduct of the Public Employment Program, counties, along with cities and the states, began to raise their voices on matters of manpower administration. A second grant of $250,000 to the County Manpower Project meant that the counties would continue to push for a larger role in control of local manpower programs.

8

STATE PROGRAMS

The states have had major roles in most pre-World War II federal grant-in-aid programs—those for highways, vocational education, welfare, health, for example. But many of the federal aid programs started between 1945 and 1970 bypassed the states and went directly to localities—programs such as urban renewal, airports, water and sewer facilities, community action, and model cities. Since the Manpower and Training Act of 1962 was to be run by "old-line" agencies, it followed the state route, but the new manpower programs of the Economic Opportunity Act of 1964 pursued a straight line to the local level.

The Public Employment Program compromised. Although the act made both local and state governments "eligible applicants," the Department of Labor, in inventing the program-agent concept, decided to deal directly with the larger cities and counties and to have the states act as agents for the remainder. The states would be invited to review and comment on the applications of city and county program agents, but they would have no approval authority. For the balance-of-state, a state agency would prepare the application and would channel funds to local subagents and employing agencies.

In addition, the Labor Department guidelines gave the states a share of Section 5 funds allocated to city and county program agents in the same proportion that state employment in the particular city or county was to total public employment. The objective was to enable state agencies to hire eligible local residents.

92

In practice, this meant that in the state capital and in cities and counties with state universities and colleges state government would control a sizable portion of emergency-employment funds (as we will see in chapter nine in the case of Champaign County, Illinois). These funds would be used for jobs with state agencies, unless the governor chose to allocate them to other eligible agencies, but persons employed had to be residents of the local area.

Thus, state government had three main responsibilities: to arrange for state jobs in all areas of the state, to distribute funds to eligible applicants in jurisdictions not served by other program agents, and to review and comment on applications of other program agents. By federal regulation, the governors were the state program agents, but they delegated this responsibility to an agency of their choosing, such as the state employment service, the personnel department, the department of community affairs, or the manpower planning unit in the governor's office. For the balance-of-state program, two states kept the funds entirely for state jobs, twelve states gave money to counties, five to municipalities, and thirty-one to both counties and municipalities. In some states, local school districts and other special districts also received funds from the state to create emergency jobs. Nine states used multicounty planning districts or councils of governments to help plan local programs outside eligible cities and counties.

North Carolina

As the Emergency Employment Act was working its way through Congress, the North Carolina legislature was considering a bill to establish a State Manpower Council. The state legislature had passed it by the time the secretary of labor announced the emergency-employment guidelines, but the governor of North Carolina had not yet appointed members to the council. Therefore, the Department of Administration, a staff arm of the governor well versed in planning and management matters and experienced in federal grantsmanship, took responsibility for preparing the state's application.[1]

In anticipation of passage of the federal program, the North

Carolina Manpower Development Corporation, a private non-profit organization governed by influential citizens and close to state government, had stimulated the formation of a task force of state-agency representatives to consider creative possibilities of PEP jobs. But the tight federal deadlines made it impossible for this task force to work fast enough to influence the state's application, which was drawn up by staff from the Department of Administration.

Of the $6.1 million in Section 5 funds allocated to North Carolina, $2.7 million was earmarked for twenty-one city and county program agents. Nineteen of these submitted their own applications, and the other two joined the state's program. The Department of Administration decided to reach the balance of the state through seventeen planning districts, which had recently been created, and in each of these it designated a coordinating organization—most often the council of governments. The application for the initial 20 percent of funds was based upon guesstimates made at the state level, but the coordinating organizations fed in proposals for jobs and agency assignments for the full funding proposal. These were put together by the Department of Administration, which also added in the state jobs to be filled in the cities and counties having their own program agents.

After the Manpower Planning Council was appointed and a staff selected, its administrator took charge of the Public Employment Program. He and his staff dealt with the coordinating organizations and through them with local employing agents.

Utah

Utah already had a State Manpower Planning Council, with nearly four years experience, when the Public Employment Program began. The council consisted of the heads of state agencies related to manpower plus public members from management, labor, minority groups, and citizens-at-large. The chairman was appointed by the governor and served as staff director, making the operation part of the governor's office.[2]

In the spring of 1971 the Manpower Planning Council began to plan how to utilize the federal emergency-employment funds, in the event the program should be approved in Washington. The council concentrated on Salt Lake County, the most populous county in the state, and conducted an inventory of job opportunities with city and county departments.

When the Emergency Employment Act became law, the council turned its attention to persuading the Labor Department to make it the one and only program agent for all of Utah. It pointed out that 85 percent of the state's population is concentrated in a four-county corridor ninety miles long and fifteen miles wide, north and south of Salt Lake City, and that this urbanized area should be dealt with as a whole rather than divided among one city and four county program agents. The Labor Department agreed to go along, provided the city and counties consented. The governor convened the heads of these units and offered to use the state's $1-million dollar share of Utah's $4-million Section 5 allocation for city and county jobs. This arrangement was agreed to, and a joint proposal was prepared, with the Manpower Planning Council handling the duties of program agent, and the city and counties signing up as subagents. In the sparsely settled balance-of-state, nine multicounty planning districts were utilized.

The Section 5 allocation to Salt Lake City and the four urban counties was already determined by the Labor Department. For the nine planning districts, the Manpower Planning Council distributed funds on the basis of unemployed veterans, giving results not much different than if total population had been used. Section 6 fund allocation was determined by the Labor Department, and Salt Lake City and thirteen counties shared in the $1.5 million earmarked for Utah.

Within the course of several months the Manpower Planning Council negotiated 187 subcontracts, including large ones with the city and counties which might have been program agents on their own. But this occurred with such speed that the preplanning of job opportunities was not worked in. Fiscal and reporting responsibilities were delegated to the state's Department of Employment Security, which has long handled such matters in other manpower programs, and in some rural areas, the department took care of other administrative details. This department was also involved in recruitment throughout the state, but participating governmental units also recruited and made the hiring decisions. To monitor local performance and offer technical assistance, the Manpower Planning Council established a unit with a director, assistant director, and a dozen coordinators. After a year, the governor transferred this unit to the Office of Community Affairs (another part of the governor's office more regularly involved in program operations), but the Manpower Planning Council retained its policy role.

Texas

In Texas the Department of Community Affairs, a brand new agency, took charge of the Public Employment Program. The department, established by the state legislature, came into being on September 1, 1971, and replaced the Division of State and Local Relations, which the governor had set up two years earlier by executive order. The federal apportionment formulas allotted $8 million for eighteen cities and fourteen counties large enough to have their own program agents, but $1 million of this amount was earmarked for state jobs in those localities. In addition, the state had $3.7 million with which to serve the other 240 counties in the balance-of-state. Texas officials, realizing that these funds would be stretched thin, vigorously protested the choice of federal formula which shortchanged Texas and benefited California, but to no avail.[3]

To cope with the state's immense territory, the Department of Community Affairs turned to twenty-four councils of governments (COG), which are located throughout the state and have voluntary membership of most counties. All twenty-four agreed to participate and proceeded to work with counties, cities, and other local-government units to identify jobs which could be filled. Each COG became a subagent, and the local jurisdictions were the employing agencies (an arrangement not anticipated in the Labor Department guidelines). About 1,300 jobs were distributed among 448 employing agents, of which 266 had only 1 position. A two-part formula, based on number and percent unemployed, was used for fund allocation.

For the state jobs, the participating departments were also treated as subagents and their field offices as employing agents. The Department of Health accounted for about half the state jobs, and other state agencies consisted of ones dealing with alcoholism, mental health, water quality, and community affairs.

Illinois

The governor's Manpower Office in Illinois assumed responsibility for preparing the application for PEP funds. This office had been established when the governor received a planning grant to participate in the Cooperative Area Manpower Planning System (CAMPS). Of the $17.9 million in Section 5 funds allotted to the state, $4.3 million was available for use outside cities and counties with their own program agents. The Manpower Office decided to allocate half the balance-of-state funds to a dozen counties in the southern part of the state, which had chronically high unemployment, and the rest was spread around to other counties. At the local level, both counties and cities filled jobs under the program.[4]

In addition, the state had $1.6 million to use for state jobs in places where city and county program agents were operating. Responsibility for recruitment and selection of participants was assigned to the Department of Personnel, which normally handles state hiring, and which for two years had been handling Public Service Careers and a special on-the-job training program. As one example, in Champaign County most of the state jobs were assigned to the University of Illinois, but some were given to other state agencies and others to county departments. Recruitment occurred through the State Employment Service.

But before many people could be employed the Illinois State Employees Union took the state to court on grounds that persons hired with PEP funds might gain special treatment not accorded regular employees. The union also complained that it had not been consulted as the legislation required. A district court issued a preliminary injunction which halted state hiring for two months but later dismissed the suit when the union was given a copy of the agreement between the state and the Labor Department.[4]

Missouri

How to handle PEP funds presented a problem to Missouri because state laws prohibited state agencies from spending funds exceeding the appropriation from the state legislature, and the legislature was not in session in August, 1971. Fortunately, the Division of Employment Security was an exception because of its participation in the federal-state employment-security system, and the governor therefore designated it to handle emergency-employment money. So as to keep the operation close to the chief executive, he appointed as emergency coordinator a person who had been working for the governor's Manpower Planning Section.[5]

Of Missouri's $13.5-million Section 5 allocation, $11.1 million was earmarked for the four cities and seven counties which could become program agents, but $1 million would be for state jobs in these 11 areas. This left $2.3 million for the balance of the state, and the governor decided to use up to a third of this amount for state jobs.

To determine what state jobs should be filled for emergency employment, the state comptroller compared agency staff requests with appropriated positions for the 1972 fiscal year and assumed that appropriations lower than the requests represented unmet needs. This became an index for assigning jobs to state agencies, and the jobs had to be filled in various parts of the state in relation to the total PEP funds allotted to each city and county.

For the balance-of-state the governor determined that eighteen regional planning commissions would serve as intermediaries between the Division of Employment Security and local governments. The state used the Labor Department's two-part formula of number and severity of unemployment to allocate funds to the districts, but it did not inform the regional-planning commissions what their share would be. Lacking such guidance, the commissions came up with proposals for some 1,200 jobs, costing over $7 million. The Division of Employment Security pared this down to $1.5 million, which produced 300 jobs for 250 cities, counties, and school districts. One subagent hired eight persons, but all the others employed five or less.

Boone County (population 81,000), which includes Columbia and the campus of the University of Missouri, was entitled to have its presiding judge serve as a program agent. But since 80 percent of the funds would go to state jobs, leaving only $17,000 for the county, the County Court voted to have the state handle the whole program and use the county as a subagent.

California

As we saw in chapter seven, the Labor Department's allocation methods benefited California most of all, and the state got $100 million, or one sixth, of the Section 5-formula funds. Of this amount, $96 million was allocated to the thirty-six cities and thirty counties which qualified as program agents, but the state could claim about $12 million for jobs with state agencies, colleges, and universities in these locales. This left $4.2 million for twenty-seven counties and some Indian reservations in the balance-of-state, which was allotted on the basis of number of unemployed and the rate of unemployment in each county.[6]

The governor designated the California Human Resources Development Department to handle the Public Employment Program. This department had come into being in 1968 to administer various manpower programs; state employment-service activities were its largest functions, and it also developed the annual CAMPS plan.

Twenty-five state agencies were assigned emergency-employment positions to fill. Ordinarily most state jobs are filled through competitive examinations administered by the State Personnel Board, but this was impracticable if hiring was to take place quickly. The solution was to utilize the governor's power to fill a certain number of exempt positions requiring no civil-service examination. This resolved the immediate problem, but it meant that PEP employees could not take promotional examinations and would have to pass an entry-level exam if they wanted to gain permanent civil-service status. But state colleges and universities in California are not subject to these civil-service requirements and thus were able to exercise greater flexibility in hiring and promotion of PEP participants.

The California Rural Legal Association, an organization funded by the U. S. Office of Economic Opportunity, felt that the state was not filling enough PEP jobs with rural unemployed and persons with limited English-speaking ability. A district court agreed and ordered the state to make extra efforts to hire these segments of the unemployed.

In the balance-of-state, the Human Resources Development Department worked through county governments.

National Governors Conference

The National Governors Conference was the third public-interest group of public officials to receive a grant from the Labor Department. This grant came in the spring of 1972, well after the Public Employment Program was underway, and its purpose was to assist governors and state manpower directors in planning and carrying out comprehensive manpower programs. Emergency employment was only incidentally within this scope, and therefore the manpower project of the National Governors Conference was much less involved in PEP than either the National League of Cities/U. S. Conference of Mayors or the National Association of Counties.

9

DEMONSTRATION PROJECTS

As the Labor Department moved quickly to disburse $600 million in formula funds under Section 5 and $250 million for areas of high unemployment under Section 6, it still had $150 million in discretionary funds left under Section 5. Some of this money would be required for federal administration, some to bolster the programs for Indians, some for migratory farm workers, and some for local areas with special problems, but this still left a large balance. If word got out that the department had such a sizable kitty of funds, political pressures would mount to influence how to spend it. But this could be avoided if the funds were soon assigned to large-scale special projects.

It happened that two ideas for such projects were perking within the federal government. Prior to passage of the Emergency Employment Act, a research unit at the Office of Economic Opportunity had been designing a demonstration project aimed at testing the economic impact of a massive public-service employment program. OEO had previously conducted a guaranteed-income demonstration in one locality, and now it wanted to see the effect of an employment approach. At the same time, California and New York wanted to introduce mandatory work requirements into the welfare system and were seeking federal permission, but within the Labor Department, staff working for the assistant secretary for policy, evaluation, and research were developing their own approach to employment aspects of welfare reform and had some notions to test. Malcolm Lovell, assistant secretary for manpower, was sympathetic to both sets of ideas—economic impact and jobs for welfare recipients—and so was his planning staff. He was also quite cognizant of the political problems which could arise if the discretionary funds were not quickly committed.

Therefore, in September the Labor Department decided to undertake two major demonstration projects—high-impact and welfare—and to allocate $115 million for this purpose. For the demonstrations to be manageable, they would have to be concentrated in a limited number of areas and states. The choice of states was made with the advice of an interdepartmental committee of assistant-secretary rank, all political appointees of the President. They selected California, Illinois, New Jersey, and New York and decided that a southern state should be the fifth state. Later they chose South Carolina.

Earlier, when the Section 5 formula favored California, members of Congress and governors and manpower officials in the losing states claimed that this was a political decision. But Labor Department officials privately responded that other states in which the Administration had a strong political interest for the 1972 presidential election were among the losers (e.g., Texas, Illinois, and New York). In the case of the demonstration projects, political considerations were stronger, for the four nonsouthern states selected all had Republican governors and were expected to produce a closely divided vote in the presidential election. South Carolina seemed promising for the Republicans, but the state's administrative competence to conduct a demonstration was also a factor.

Once the states were chosen, a working group from two offices within the Manpower Administration, the Planning, Evaluation and Research office and the Public Service Employment office, developed a list of prospective locales. For the high-impact projects, they decided to deal with entire labor markets, and not merely the jurisdiction of a single city or county program agent, if the labor area were larger, and they wanted relatively isolated labor markets to avoid movement of labor force from nearby areas. They wished to provide enough jobs to reach 10 to 15 percent of the unemployed, and they wanted enough projects to enable them to try several variations. These factors meant that the largest metropolitan labor markets would have to be excluded because of high cost. For the welfare projects, they desired places with sizable welfare rolls and high concentrations of unemployed.

On October 8, Secretary of Labor Hodgson announced the two demonstration projects and the localities chosen.[1] The $65 million high-impact demonstration would be conducted in a dozen areas in the five states, and the $50 million welfare demonstration would be carried out in eleven areas in four of the states and in several California sites yet to be chosen. Simultaneously, Republican congressmen and senators from those states announced the projects for their localities.

High-Impact Projects

The demonstration design for the high-impact projects called for two basic models. Model 1 would add enough funds to the existing Public Employment Program in the area to provide jobs for about 10 percent of the unemployed. Model 2 would expand public employment in a few communities to absorb 15 percent of the unemployed in the first year and 25 percent in the second year.

Three variations were also envisioned. Variation A would test the effect of concentrating on jobs for the disadvantaged. This would be done by requiring that at least 75 percent of the enrollees be unemployed or underemployed persons with incomes below the poverty level. Variation B would examine the effect of limiting the wage level. This would be accomplished by requiring that the wage of at least 90 percent of enrollees not exceed some maximum level, such as the average public-employment wage in the community selected. Variation C would investigate problems typical of low-wage areas, and this would be implemented in two southern communities. Table II shows the labor market areas selected for these models and variations.

Administration of the high-impact projects would be handled by the same apparatus as the regular program. This meant that the program agents operating in the different areas would run the local projects and that the regional offices of the Manpower Administration would receive and process applications for project funds.

TABLE II

*Labor-Market Areas for High-Impact Demonstration Projects,
by Model, Combination, and Amount of Funds ($ in millions)*

	Model 1 Impact: 10% of Unemployed	Model 2 Impact: 15% of Unemployed in 1st year, 25% in 2nd year
Basic Model	San Diego Co., Ca. ($17.2) Atlantic Co., N.J. ($3.3) Syracuse SMSA, N.Y. ($9.3)	Springfield SMSA, Ill. ($5.4) Decatur SMSA, Ill. ($2.9)
Variation A Restrict 75% of enrollment to poor unemployed or underemployed.	Champaign-Urbana SMSA, Ill. ($1.7) Elmira-Chemung County, New York ($1.5)	
Variation B Restrict wage level of 90% of enrollment to average of public employment in community selected.	Riverside-San Bernardino SMSA, Ca. ($12.8) Jefferson Co., N.Y. ($1.2)	Trenton SMSA, N.J. ($6.7)
Variation C Model 1 in southern community with low wages, high poverty.	Columbia SMSA, S.C. ($2.4) Spartanburg County S.C. ($1.6)	

Local officials in *Decatur, Illinois* were pleasantly surprised to learn that their area had been chosen to receive an additional $2.9 million for emergency employment. State government would get nearly a million for state jobs, but the $1.95 million allocated to the city was more than ten times previous grants for Section 5 and Section 6 programs. The city manager's assistant once again worked with city departments and other local agencies to prepare a list of jobs and to draw up an application for City Council approval. City agencies took about 60 percent of the new jobs, the School District a tenth, and the rest were divided among the Park District, Sanitary District, Junior College, Housing Authority, and Public Library.[2]

Since many of the agencies were unionized, the local unions were notified of their right to comment on the grant application but were asked to agree to only eleven days advance notice, rather than the fifteen required, in order to speed up the applications. The unions agreed, and questions about recruitment methods raised by two unions were easily resolved. Then the application was hand delivered to the Chicago regional office.

The most serious objection raised came from the Decatur Education Association, which claimed that fourteen teachers fired by the School District during a strike were eligible for emergency employment. The city maintained that this was not relevant to approval of the grant for demonstration funds. The Labor Department concurred and approved the application. Because the city had contacted unions in advance, the issue raised in the court injunction obtained by the Illinois State Employees' Union(related in chapter eleven) did not delay the Decatur program.

The city and the other employing agents began hiring with high-impact funds on December 1. Thenceforth, high-impact, Section 5, and Section 6 programs were blended together as a single operation.

The pleasure felt by officials in *Champaign County, Illinois* on hearing about the $1.7 million in high-impact funds to be sent their way by the Labor Department soon turned to chagrin when they learned that a minimum of 75 percent of the jobs had to be filled with disadvantaged persons. Then they discovered that the state would take $1.2 million as the major governmental employer in the county. For administrative reasons, the $125,000 previously allotted under Section 5 would be combined with the new funds and would operate under high-impact guidelines, including the 75 percent disadvantaged requirement.[3]

Notwithstanding their concern, local public officials got busy preparing an application. A meeting at the county supervisor's office brought together representatives of all local governmental units, and an EEA advisory council was formed consisting of the mayors of Champaign, Urbana, and Rantoul and representatives of state government, the University of Illinois, and the County Board of

Supervisors. As it had done for the Section 5 program, the Champaign County Regional Planning Commission conducted a survey of job possibilities and wrote the application, which was dispatched to the Labor Department regional office.

But unlike Decatur, Champaign County did not circulate its application among labor unions, and after the district court enjoined the state Public Employment Program over the same issue, the Labor Department held back its approval of the Champaign County high-impact application until the unions had had a chance to comment. This delayed hiring for jobs with county and local governmental agencies until January. Once they got going, the requirement that three-fourths of the positions be filled with disadvantaged persons was met without difficulty.

Filling the state jobs took even longer because of an argument between the University of Illinois and the State Personnel Department over the allocation of positions. Although the university accounted for 90 percent of state employment in the county, it was first given only 40 of the 152 new state jobs, while the patronage-prone Department of Conservation, with no facilities in the county, was assigned 44. The university protested, and after a while its allotment was raised to 60 and then finally to 102, and the Conservation Department was excluded. But before the university could employ anyone, it had to clear up a dispute with the electrical-workers union over whether persons hired under the Public Employment Program would displace laid-off union members. The university pledged that, for the most part, it would be filling different kinds of jobs, but that it would rehire laid-off personnel where possible. Meanwhile, the state moved slowly to fill the other state jobs because of requirements for a civil-service examination before hiring so that the state departments lagged five months behind county and city agencies. When finally underway, the state and university jobs were not much different under the high-impact program than were the jobs under Section 5.

Elsewhere, the high-impact program was also folded into the regular Public Employment Program under the mayor, the county commissioners, the city manager, or the personnel department. Likewise, the selection of subagents and jobs followed a process similar to that for Section 5, whereby the central administrative agency made determinations based upon job requests and judgment of relative need. The jobs were mostly entry-level positions because of pressures from labor unions, the expectation that the program would not last long, and the desire to hire the disadvantaged.[4]

Welfare Projects

The demonstration design for the the welfare projects envisioned five models consisting of different combinations of two variables: the amount of support services and the participation requirement. Low support services would consist of only child care and transportation subsidies, while high support services would add counseling, job coaching, medical aid, education, and occupational training. Participation might be mandatory, requiring that an employable individual who could not be placed in an unsubsidized job or training program must take a public-employment job or be penalized by loss of welfare benefits. In contrast, participation might be voluntary so that an individual could refuse a public-employment job without penalty. A variation would combine low support and mandatory participation with work-relief projects, which New York was already operating. These models and the places where they were to be applied are shown in Table III.

These projects were to be tied to the existing welfare program, and funds from the Emergency Employment Act would be pooled with regular welfare funds. This meant that the Department of Health, Education and Welfare (HEW) would have to be a major partner in the demonstration and would, indeed, be the channel of project funding. This required HEW to follow the procedures of Section 1115 of the Social Security Act in granting waivers of law and regulations to permit the demonstration to function. Such a partnership between the Labor Department and HEW was a continuation of working relationships developed under the Work Incentive Program (WIN) established by the Social Security Amendments of 1967. Within the Labor Department, the Office of Employment Development Programs, which had responsibility for WIN, took charge of the welfare demonstration rather than the

Office of Public Service Employment, but the latter was involved in program design, as were the Office of Economic Opportunity and the Office of Management and Budget.

TABLE III

Labor-Market Areas for Welfare-Demonstration Projects by Models and Amount of Funds

	Demonstration Model		Amount (in millions)	
Labor-Market Area	Supportive Services	Participation	1st Yr.	2nd Yr.
Illinois				
Chicago	High	Voluntary	$7.0	$2.1
East St. Louis	High & Low	Voluntary	4.0	1.2
Moline/Rock Island	Low	Voluntary	1.0	.3
New Jersey				
Camden	Low	Voluntary	2.5	.7
Newark	High	Voluntary	4.0	1.2
Paterson	High	Voluntary	1.5	.4
New York City				
Harlem	Low	Mandatory + work relief	6.0	1.5
Brooklyn	Low	Mandatory		
Bergen	High	Mandatory		
South Carolina				
Charleston	High & Low	Mandatory	.8	.2
Greenville	Low	Mandatory	.8	.2
Horry County	Low	Mandatory	.2	.1
Orangeburg	High	Voluntary	.2	.1

Since federal welfare funds go to state government, the participating states had to serve as program agents for the demonstration projects and had to add state welfare money to the fund pool. The state could funnel wage payment funds to local employment agencies, such as city and county government, but any supplemental welfare benefits and social services would go through the regular welfare system, which is state operated in some places and delegated to counties elsewhere. In essence, this made the welfare demonstration a three-way partnership between the Labor Department, HEW, and state government. Because of the resulting complications, the first local program was not underway until April, 1972.[5]

In *Illinois*, the welfare-demonstration project was planned by a special task force attached to the Governor's Manpower Office, but administration was turned over to the State Employment Service, assisted by the Department of Public Aid (the two departments running WIN). In Chicago, designing the project involved the same officials who had prepared the Section 5 and Section 6 programs, i.e., the Mayor's Office of Manpower and the Personnel Department of the Civil Service Commission. Once again, they brought in the Board of Education, Park District, and other independent government agencies. The local office of the State Employment Service participated in the planning, as did the Cook County Department of Public Aid. But it was the Governor's Office of Manpower which took care of negotiations with the U. S. Labor Department.

The pool of jobs available for the regular Chicago program was used for the welfare demonstration. Eligible participants were enrollees of the state's Work Incentive Program (WIN), which was run by the State Employment Service, and all WIN enrollees were persons referred by the Cook County Department of Public Aid. As the program got going, the WIN offices were at first producing thirty eligible referrals a day, but after a few weeks the number fell as the pool of persons judged to be job ready dwindled. Moreover, many of the referrals lacked the skills required for clerical occupations which many WIN participants had presumably been trained for; therefore, the occupational mix had to be changed to a lower skill level. Because of these factors, the welfare-demonstration project in Chicago moved more slowly than the regular Public Employment Program did.

But the city moved faster than Cook County, which also served as a subagent for the welfare demonstration. A third subagent also functioned in the Chicago area: Malcolm X College, which managed a consortium of fifteen neighborhood organizations on the Westside. Elsewhere in Illinois, East St. Louis participated and made the demonstration a responsibility of the local Department of

Urban Affairs, and in Rock Island a county task force handled the special welfare project.

In *South Carolina*, the welfare demonstration was planned by the Manpower and Organizational Development Office, functioning under the governor. When the director of this unit became head of a new Department of Administration, he continued his overall responsibility for the demonstration but assigned it to the Office of Social Development. What this meant was that two old-line agencies, the Department of Public Welfare and the State Employment Service, would be subordinate to the governor's office, a move resisted by these agencies but supported by public-interest organizations seeking a better welfare system in the state. Although the demonstration was state administered, selected cities and counties served as subagents.

In *New Jersey*, the EEA coordinator in the Department of Labor and Industry was the officer in charge, but the Department of Public Welfare was also involved. Operations were directed through county welfare departments, and in Newark the mayor's manpower director had a role.

In *New York*, the Department of Labor nominally ran the program, but since the demonstration operated only in New York City, that city's Human Resources Administration did most of the planning and administration, with planning involvement of the EEA Task Force in the mayor's office. (Elsewhere in New York, the state's own "workfare" program embarked upon an effort to provide mandatory employment for welfare recipients capable of work.)

In *California*, the demonstration got tangled with the governor's intention to have his own work relief program, and it never got going along the lines of the demonstration design, though some of the federal money went for support of the California plan.

What happened once these high-impact and welfare-demonstration projects got underway is reviewed in chapter fifteen.

10

CIVIL SERVICE AND
PUBLIC-EMPLOYEE
UNIONS

As the Public Employment Program got into operation in localities and states, it encountered two strong institutional forces affecting the hiring and assignment of public employees: civil-service systems and employee unions. Civil-service systems operate under state laws and regulations and under municipal charters, ordinances, and rules, and the commissions and personnel departments which run them are generally accustomed "to going by the book." Public-employee unions constitute the most rapidly expanding segment of organized labor, and as they have gained in strength they have become quite assertive of their members' interests. Something new and different such as Public Employment Program inevitably challenged these forces, and between them civil-service systems and employee unions significantly affected the course of emergency employment.

Civil-Service Requirements

The Emergency Employment Act requires that agencies and institutions receiving financial assistance must give assurances that they will undertake analysis of job descriptions and a reevaluation of skill requirements at all levels of employment, and that they will seek to eliminate artificial barriers to employment and occupational advancement, including any civil-service requirements which restrict employment opportunities for the disadvantaged. These provisions were inserted with the intent of promoting civil-service reform.

111

The act specified that the secretary of labor should promulgate regulations to implement these provisions. To comply with the requirement, the regulations published in the Federal Register on August 14, 1971, stated that this would be done in accordance with guidelines issued by the U. S. Civil Service Commission. These guidelines came out in September and dealt with such topics as job descriptions and job structure, qualifications for jobs, recruitment methods, examining and selecting applicants, training, and management practices.[1]

In the meantime, the Labor Department had asked the National Civil Service League, then in its ninetieth year as a private organization dedicated to effective public-personnel systems, to prepare recommendations on how civil service could be adapted to the needs and realities of this new program. Accordingly, the league published a report entitled *Emergency Action Plan for Public Service Employment* (August, 1971). This report gave consideration to the following basic factors:

Identification of the kinds and numbers of positions to be used.

Knowledge of the characteristics of the eligible participants.

Priorities among the potential positions that meet program requirements for employment of the unemployed and underemployed.

Job standards and qualification requirements that provide a desirable "match" between the participants and the public service positions established for transitional employment.

Choice of civil-service or other public-employment procedures that permit the quickest screening, examination, and hiring to meet identified priorities in terms of specific designations of the unemployed and underemployed participants, and public-service needs.

Expediting the administrative process involved in the recruiting, screening, selection and organizational placement of transitional public-service employees.

The league's report considered each factor and presented sample provisions from local and state regulations which seemed appropriate for handling civil-service issues in emergency employment.[2]

Then in November, 1971, the Labor Department arranged for the U. S. Civil Service Commission to remain involved by devising methods for state and county civil-service systems to change unnecessary personnel requirements, to convert temporary jobs to career appointments, and to otherwise facilitate transition to permanent jobs. With funds transferred from the department, the Civil Service Commission established a staff position in each regional office to carry out these responsibilities.

Local Experience with Civil Service

How these civil-service issues were resolved in actuality can be observed by reviewing the experience of several localities.

Recapitulation. Chapters nine and ten related how a sample of city and county programs unfolded and noted that in the majority of cases civil service was a factor to contend with. New York City has a tightly prescribed civil-service system, and the emergency jobs had to be filled through provisional appointment of persons who could qualify for permanent civil-service status. Chicago has a much looser system, which in practice permits provisional appointments for indefinite periods, so that there were few civil-service obstacles to hiring for this program. Milwaukee's civil service is extensive in coverage, but its formal-education requirements are not nearly so rigid as New York's and disadvantaged persons could be hired more readily. San Diego first overcame its "rule-of-three" certification requirements through a hiring-hall procedure, and the City Council later amended the rules to permit selective certification for PEP jobs. Decatur kept these jobs out of the regular civil-service system but gave preference points to participants toward future city jobs. Laredo also kept most jobs outside civil service, and when the city faced challenges to policemen's and firemen's positions under civil service, it dropped such jobs from the program. San Diego County bypassed the civil-service system completely by setting up a schedule of temporary jobs with no prospect for tenure. As for the other cities and counties considered in the previous chapters, no formal civil-service system existed in Winston-Salem; Robeson County, North Carolina; Bell County, Kentucky; Champaign County, Illinois; and the four counties in South Texas.

The experience of three other cities studied by the National League of Cities/U. S. Conference of Mayors—Baltimore, Maryland; Birmingham, Alabama; and Compton, California—provide further illustrations about civil service and emergency employment.[8]

Baltimore. The Mayor's Office of Manpower Resources took responsibility for the Public Employment Program in Baltimore, Maryland (population 906,000). This was a unit first established to handle manpower planning and provide staff services to the Manpower Area Planning Council. It decided to classify PEP jobs as temporary, noncivil-service positions but to relate them directly to existing civil-service positions so that participants could have an opportunity to meet permanent job specifications within six months to a year of employment.

This would not be easy because the fifty-year-old job-classification system in Baltimore's civil service had over 2,000 job titles, each tailored to the desires of different municipal departments. Each job classification had its own pay scale, tests, career ladder, and eligibility and promotional lists. City officials had been concerned about this inefficient system, which was expensive and cumbersome to operate, and which inhibited recruitment and upward and lateral job mobility of city employees. The temporary jobs under the Public Employment Program gave the city an opportunity to develop a new approach—one based on generic classification of jobs.

Accordingly, eight job classifications were established for emergency employment: clerical-service employee, community-service employee, educational-service employee, environmental-service employee, equipment–operations–and–maintenance employee, health-service employee, planning employee, and public-protection employee. Within each classification, a participant was assigned to one of five levels based upon criteria related to education, experience, and skill.

With this experience under its belt, Baltimore then applied for a grant under the Intergovernmental Personnel Act to extend generic classification to the city's entire civil-service system.

Birmingham. The mayor's manpower staff in Birmingham, Alabama (population 301,000) developed the application for PEP funds and intended to administer the program itself. This did not happen, however, because the Jefferson County Personnel Board insisted on handling program administration. This board was established by state law to operate a merit system for all cities in Jefferson County having 5,000 or more residents, of which there are a dozen besides Birmingham. It maintains a register of eligible applicants, and for each vacancy in a city job it supplies the top three candidates from the register.

Birmingham gave top priority to public-service needs in law enforcement, fire protection, and public works and requested the Personnel Board for persons to fill such positions as police patrolman, fireman, and maintenance mechanic helper. The board was able to screen the eligible list for unemployed persons in order of ranking, but by its rules it was unable to apply a residency requirement. Since Birmingham's PEP funds had to be used to hire residents of the city, this prevented hiring for jobs to which nonresidents were referred, and the funds had to be reassigned to other positions.

However, the merit system included a general classification for "public-service aide," a trainee position which had never been utilized. This was activated and used to hire persons who otherwise would not have been eligible for civil-service jobs. For the Section 6 program, most of the jobs were low-skill and were placed in the unclassified service, thus providing greater hiring flexibility.

Some of Birmingham's PEP funds were assigned to the Board of Education and to Jefferson State Junior College, both of which have relatively flexible personnel systems. Their jobs could be adapted more easily to the needs of the unemployed than the positions under the Jefferson County Personnel Board.

Compton. Located in Los Angeles County, Compton, California (population 77,000) has a council-manager form of government. The application for PEP funds was prepared by the staff of the Model Cities Program, which was experienced in writing federal proposals, and which had been operating its own manpower programs. The city's Personnel Office developed information on what jobs should be accorded priority, and it took charge of recruitment when the program got underway.

Compton has a strong civil-service system which applies to most regular jobs. Eligible lists are based upon written and oral examinations administered by Los Angeles County, working under contract with the city. But for PEP jobs Compton decided to utilize only the position of police officer in the classified service, and this job was filled through the regular procedures for recruitment and examination.

For the other jobs, the City Council passed a resolution creating a "project contract position," a temporary job not part of classified civil service but accorded the same benefits except tenure and promotional rights. This made it possible to establish a special eligible list of persons for whom PEP jobs were intended, but it left unresolved the problem of how to bring these persons into regular employment.

City Council handled this transition problem by adopting a resolution which permitted PEP participants who successfully passed a civil-service examination to have priority over all other applicants on related open-competitive lists, though not over other employees on promotional eligible lists. This meant that participants would be competing for regular jobs only among themselves, and this was a strong incentive for effective performance in emergency employment.

Labor Unions: Legislation and Guidelines

As noted in chapter three, the AFL-CIO was active and influential in the campaign for enactment of the Emergency Employment Act. This was an expression of labor's political and economic philosophy, which favors public-service jobs as a means of achieving fuller employment in the United States. The concern was shared by several national unions of public employees, which were also interested in maintaining and increasing the employment level in their respective spheres of influence.

Labor lobbyists also wanted to protect union interests as the program unfolded, and they were able to get the following language into the legislation:

> Where a labor organization represents employees who are engaged in similar work in the same area to that proposed under any program for which an application is being developed for submission under this Act, such organization shall be notified and afforded a reasonable period of time in which to make comments to the applicant and to the Secretary.[4]

When the Labor Department issued its guidelines, it stated that the time allowed for comment would be fifteen days.

National Labor Organizations

Kenneth Young, the AFL-CIO lobbyist who was fully involved in legislative action, remained on the scene as these guidelines were being drawn up. He called a meeting of concerned unions and participated in several sessions with Labor Department officials on guidelines. Also involved were staff from the AFL-CIO's Human Resources Development Institute (HRDI), which became the clearing house for the expression of organized labor's concerns on emergency-employment issues as the program unfolded.

HRDI was established in 1968 through a grant from the Labor Department for the purpose of encouraging local union participation in a program called JOBS (Jobs in the Private Sector). This grant was a counterpart to one given to the National Alliance of Businessmen. Over the months, HRDI's program interests expanded to include apprenticeship programs, the Neighborhood Youth Corps, the Job Corps, and the Work Incentive Program for welfare recipients. By 1973 it had job development and placement units operating in fifty-three cities to help get disadvantaged persons into jobs under union contracts.

Along with HRDI staff, other participants in the meetings with Labor Department officials included representatives of the American Federation of State, County, and Municipal Employees (AFSCME), the International Association of Fire Fighters, the American Federation of Teachers, the Service Employees International Union, and the Laborers' International Union. These meetings took up such matters as the allocation formula, the notice requirement for union review of program agents' applications, and the rule requiring a thirty-day layoff before a public employee could be rehired in an emergency job. Union leaders objected to the last provision in particular, since seven days out-of-work was all the regulations required for other unemployed applicants, but at the time they could get no modification of the rule.

As the program got underway, HRDI maintained its interest in the Public Employment Program, but most of the action shifted to local unions, supported by their headquarters in Washington. AFSCME, with the most members, was the most active. It sent its affiliated local unions a policy guide which analyzed the Emergency Employment Act and discussed what local unions could do in different situations that might arise. As issues came up, the national federation supported its local affiliates and in some instances contacted officials in the Labor Department. The national staff of AFSCME was involved in a number of the disputes described in the case illustrations which follow. The same was true of headquarters staff of the Fire Fighters, the second most active union in this program.

Local Experience with Labor Unions

Around the country, labor-union involvement was an important factor in implementation of the Public Employment Program. Several examples can illustrate this experience.

Recapitulation. Among the cities reviewed in chapter nine, employees' unions were the strongest by far in New York, where they used their considerable bargaining power to direct a fourth of the emergency jobs for rehiring laid-off employees, particularly teachers, and to restrict other jobs to entry-level positions which would not compete with promotional opportunities of current employees. Municipal unions in Milwaukee were concerned about rehiring procedures, and suitable arrangements were amicably negotiated. In Decatur, the unions feared that the program would be used to fill civil-service jobs being eliminated because of budgetary problems, but they were reassured that this would not occur.

Among the six states discussed in chapter eleven, Illinois had the greatest controversy with unions, arising in part from poor communications. The Illinois State Employees Union complained that it had not been given the required opportunity to comment on the state's application, and it went to court to prevent special treatment for persons hired with emergency-employment funds. After a preliminary injunction halted state hiring for two months, the two parties came into fuller communications and eventually the issues were resolved out of court.

The Temple Study. Further observations on the impact of public-employee unions come from a study of eight cities made by the Center for Labor and Manpower Studies of Temple University. The study found that, generally, local unions favored the Public Employment Program, and although they raised a number of questions about individual projects, unions did not oppose the basic program concepts:

> Most often, unions were concerned with possible preferential treatment being given to PEP participants at the expense of regular employees. Such possibilities arose if the unions felt that: (1) PEP hires were substituting for regular workers; (2) PEP jobs at above-entry levels deprived regular workers of promotion opportunities; (3) normal hiring standards were waived for PEP participants; or (4) PEP workers remained working while regular employees were laid off for lack of work. Unions were also concerned with proper notification of project funding applications so that they would have the opportunity to comment and influence the project design. In several instances union involvement facilitated program implementation.[5]

Three cases from the Temple study indicate how these issues were handled in specific cities.

Detroit. As a major industrial center where labor unions are strong and politically influential, Detroit, Michigan (population 1,511,000) has a long history of collective bargaining between city government and forty-two local unions representing municipal employees. In developing the PEP plan, city officials tried to anticipate problems which might arise with the unions. As a result, they assigned most of the PEP funds to entry-level positions. As required, the city gave unions related to the proposed jobs an opportunity to comment on the application, but none filed formal comments. The fire-fighters union was not asked for comments because fire-safety jobs were call-backs. The police union was also not contacted because the proposed positions of patrolmen trainees were not covered by union contracts. The AFSCME local was apprehensive of the program and participated in three meetings with city officials to clear up its concern that PEP employees might gain preferential treatment. As the program developed, the AFSCME used established grievance procedures to successfully press the cases of several regular employees who wanted to bid for above-entry jobs created by PEP funds.[6]

Detroit's Public Employment Program got underway quite slowly. First, the city tried to get a waiver of the requirement for 10 percent matching funds because of the city's poor financial condition, but the Labor Department helped the city identify in-kind matching contributions. Then, civil-service red tape in examinations and certification slowed hiring. By January, 1972, the fiscal crisis deepened, and the city was faced with the necessity of sizable layoffs. Union leaders joined the mayor in a trip to Washington to ask the secretary of labor for a waiver of the thirty-day requirement between layoff and enrollment in emergency employment; the waiver was denied. Local negotiations led to the laying off of 250 regular employees and 109 emergency-employment participants and the rehiring of all of them, after thirty days, under the Public Employment Program. On the whole, the mutual respect of union leaders and city officials enabled Detroit to make necessary adjustments to the concerns of public-employee unions.

Louisville. Collective bargaining between the city and public-employee unions commenced more recently in Louisville, Kentucky (population 361,000), where the first union contracts with fire and police unions came in 1968, and contracts with three other unions followed. In preparing the application for PEP funds, the manpower-planning coordinator in the mayor's office called in union leaders to discuss the program with them. The union representatives registered objections to hiring above the entry level, and the proposal was modified to eliminate this problem in departments involving unionized employees. In a letter to union leaders, the manpower-planning coordinator assured them that union contracts would apply to emergency employees, and this seemed to satisfy most of the union leadership.[7]

The exception was the leadership of the International Association of Fire Fighters' local. Relations between the city and the fire-fighters union had been stormy in the past, and during the most recent contract negotiations, the fire fighters had twice gone out on strike. Whether because of this or merely by oversight, the manpower-planning coordinator failed to invite leaders from this union to the planning meeting. As a result, the fire-fighters union filed a complaint with the Labor Department that it had not been consulted and objected to three specific aspects of the Louisville Public Employment Program. The first was the use of PEP funds for civilian employees to fill three of six positions on the arson squad, jobs previously held by uniformed firemen who had passed promotional examinations. The second related to nine fire-department employees hired in September, 1971, placed on the regular payroll, and transferred to the PEP payroll a month later. The third was the use of PEP funds to provide fire and rescue protection to the airport.

The fire fighters' complaint brought representatives of the Labor Department to town. The matter of the nine employees was cleared up when the city demonstrated that a clerical error had assigned them to the wrong payroll; moreover, they would have an opportunity to become regular employees when jobs opened (which subsequently happened). The arson-squad issue dragged on for months. When the regional staff from the Department of Labor failed to take action, the fire fighters appealed directly to Washington, but with no discernible results. Finally they considered filing a grievance under union-contract procedures but hesitated doing so because it was not clear that this case was covered by contract provisions. The three civilians remained in the jobs, but the city indicated that henceforth fire fighters would have a chance for these positions through promotional examinations. Likewise, no change was made in the airport fire unit (which provided no jobs to union members anyway). All these disputes arose as much from personality clashes and a history of bad relationships as from problems inherent in the Public Employment Program.

Wilmington. Prior to enactment of the Emergency Employment Act, three events had occurred in Wilmington, Delaware (population 80,000) which affected program implementation there. In 1970, the city had started a Public Service Careers training program which had jobs at varied skill levels; originally these positions were intended for unemployed persons, but after negotiation with the local AFSCME union present employees were given first option on jobs above entry level. In the spring of 1971, the city had put into effect recommendations from the National Civil Service League to facilitate hiring and upgrading of minority employees, a matter in which city practices had been deficient. And in June, 1971, the mayor had instituted a job freeze because of an unexpected budgetary deficit.[8]

The upgrading question came up again in the Public Employment Program. Many meetings were held between city officials and AFSCME representatives, and the latter protested to the Labor Department and threatened a strike. Finally, the city agreed to give present employees five days to bid on all upgrade jobs; if an employee qualified, his or her present job would be filled by a PEP participant. The city further consented to lift its job freeze and to pay the difference in wages arising from the resulting promotion.

Minority hiring became an issue in the city's 260-man Fire Department, which prior to 1971 had only one black and one Spanish-speaking person. As it had previously done in Public Service Careers, the city bypassed normal testing procedures in order to recruit more minority personnel. The local fire-fighters union at first gave verbal approval to the Public Employment Program, but in January, 1972, it raised objections to these hiring procedures. However, the city stood firm and continued the special recruitment procedures.

Conclusions. Based on its study of these three cases and five others, the Center for Labor and Manpower Studies at Temple University concluded:

Perhaps the most significant factor in determining the method and the substance of problem resolution has been the tenor of relations between a union and the employer, the PEP program agent. . . . If the relationships were firmly established and based on mutual respect, problems associated with PEP would be resolved in the course of normal procedures, with both sides seeking an acceptable solution. If the relationship were essentially mistrustful, the PEP problems would present new opportunities for the parties to clash and aggravate existing hostilities. If the relationships did not really exist, the PEP project would not become the basis for establishing meaningful labor-management relationships and collective bargaining. Thus, PEP projects provided additional subjects for bargaining but did not change existing relationships. Instead, the manner of union involvement tended to reflect the union-management relationship in the particular situation.[9]

Thus we see that, like many other aspects of the Public Employment Program, relations between cities and labor unions were shaped by local circumstances and that considerable variation occurred throughout the nation. The same was true of civil-service systems and the ways in which they adapted to this new federal program.

PART THREE
PROGRAM RESULTS

11

INFORMATION SYSTEM, MONITORING, AND EVALUATION

One challenge facing any program funded by the national government and carried out by state and local governments is to keep track of what is happening as the program progresses. The federal department responsible for administration watches over grantees to determine whether they are achieving program objectives and whether they are spending funds properly. Congress wants to know whether its intentions are being carried out. And private organizations with an interest in the program are concerned about results.

And so it was with the Public Employment Program. The Department of Labor, Congress, and private organizations undertook, by various means, to obtain information, monitor performance, and evaluate results.

Information System

Reports from state and local grantees to federal agencies have long been part of the federal grant-in-aid system, but the advent of computers, making possible analysis of vast amounts of data, has heightened federal interest in operating statistics. So during the last ten years new management-information systems have come into being with the federal departments. The Labor Department has one which obtains reports on every individual participant in all federally assisted manpower programs across the land. It is run by the Office of Financial and Management Information Systems (OFMIS), which is a part of the Manpower Administration.

127

Naturally, the Labor Department wanted to extend its information system to the Public Employment Program. The newly created Office of Public Service Employment needed program information on what far-flung grantees were doing. And the political executives in the department had to know what was happening, for they were being pressed by White House staff for regular progress reports on how fast states and localities were hiring unemployed persons for the new jobs.

A working group on reports was one of the first of four work groups set up by the Office of Public Service Employment in July, 1971. It consisted of staff from that office and from OFMIS. In addition, the department contracted with a private firm, Macro Systems, Inc., for assistance in the design of the data system. The product of this effort was a sixty-page booklet setting forth an Agent Information System.[1] The system was built upon three basic reports to be filled out by program agents. The first report was a participant-information record designed to show the basic socioeconomic profile of each individual entering the program, previous work experience, assignment in emergency employment, and at termination, the kind of job taken or other status if unemployed. The other two reports, which were to be completed monthly by each program agent and large subagent, were a summary of participant characteristics and a report on enrollment, termination, and financial matters. All three reports went to the regional offices of the Labor Department and from there on to Washington, where OFMIS entered the first and third reports into a computer. OFMIS then produced a series of computer print-outs for use by the Office of Public Service Employment and the regional offices.

Program Monitoring

In addition to the program overview provided by computer data analysis, the Labor Department was interested in the accomplishments of individual program agents. The regional offices, which ordinarily bear the basic responsibilities for this task, have field personnel assigned to oversee a variety of manpower programs in specific localities, and when the Public Employment Program came along, it was added to their assignment. The regional staff examined the monthly reports received from program agents and made regular field visits to verify information and confer with program-agent staff and others in the community.

In addition, some personnel in the national Office of Public Service Employment had part-time assignments watching over programs in particular regions, and they tried to examine semiannually the reports of the largest program agents and annually the reports of smaller program agents, subagents, and employing agents.

Auditing

Financial review was handled by the Labor Department's Office of Program Review and Audit, which is under the direction of the assistant secretary for administration and thus is independent of the Manpower Administration. This office has its own crew of auditors who have the right to review expenditures made by program agents, subagents, and employing agents. As the Public Employment Program was getting underway, the office supplemented its own staff by contracting with private accounting firms and state auditing agencies to determine whether program agents and subagents had an adequate accounting system and accounting personnel and whether use of funds conformed to the grant agreement. They also checked to see if state and local governments were complying with the maintenance-of-effort provisions of the law, that is, whether the program produced an actual increase in employment and not a substitution for jobs previously paid by other funds.

As a further check, the General Accounting Office, an arm of Congress which conducts postaudits independent from those of the Executive Branch, undertook this task for PEP.

Evaluation by the Department of Labor

Beyond day-to-day and month-to-month monitoring of program agents and subagents, the Department of Labor arranged for longer-term evaluative studies. The following eight contracts were paid mainly from PEP funds; the first four were awarded through competitive bids and the others through sole-source negotiations.

Westat, Inc., was hired to check the validity of reports produced by the Agent Information System and to conduct a longitudinal study of program participants.[2] Westat interviewed approximately four thousand participants in about a hundred sites to determine whether their characteristics were correctly recorded by program agents. The firm later conducted three additional waves of interviews, over a two year period, with three sample groups of participants, to determine changes resulting from involvement in the program.

Two outside evaluators studied the demonstration projects. The National Planning Association (NPA) explored the results of the high-impact project to determine how the local projects affected public agencies, the participants, and the local economy.[3] The Auerbach Corporation undertook an assessment of the welfare demonstration to determine whether public employment was a feasible adjunct to welfare in terms of increasing employability and reducing welfare dependency. These two studies utilized the results of participant interviews obtained by a third contractor, Decision Making Information, Inc. (DMI). Auerbach dropped out after two years and DMI, assisted by Camil Associates, completed the welfare-demonstration evaluation.[4] In addition to PEP money, funds from the Economic Opportunity Act (EOA) supported the NPA study, and funds from the Work Incentive Program (WIN) paid for part of the Auerbach study.

The Labor Department arranged for the other four contracts without competitive bids. One was with the Bureau of the Census to conduct base-line surveys in the localities of the high-impact and welfare demonstration projects. (Some EOA funds went into this contract, too.) The other three were negotiated with minority-controlled firms, under the provisions of Regulation A-8 of the Office of Management and Budget. Automated Services, Inc. made a special study of termination of participants in order to supplement other data sources on what was happening. J. A. Reyes Associates, Inc. studied the institutional impact of the Public Employment Program on local jurisdictions, to determine particularly whether new types of jobs were being created and whether there were any differ-

No results of studies! evaluation?

ences in the makeup of public employment after PEP.[5] American Indian Consultants conducted an evaluation of the Indian program.[6]

Other Labor Department funds went into research related to the Public Employment Program. These came through the Manpower Administration's Office of Policy, Evaluation and Research (OPER) in the form of grants to private organizations. This was done because of OPER's interest in the broader implications of emergency employment for the design of future manpower and employment programs. One grant went to the Center for Labor and Manpower Studies at Temple University for a study of the impact of emergency employment on public-employee unions.[7] Another went to the National Civil Service League,[8] with a subgrant to the Center for Governmental Studies (Washington, D. C.),[9] for studies related to transitional employment. A third went to a University of California professor to explore alternative forms of public-service employment—their costs and benefits, their impact on poor people, their effect upon jobs in the private sector, and their influence on the alleged inflation-unemployment trade-off. Finally, the department's contract with the National League of Cities/U. S. Conference of Mayors was expanded to provide for a study of PEP in cities.

Congressional Evaluation

Members of Congress and the congressional committees which sponsor legislation are interested in its implementation, but on the whole Congress has a spotty performance in systematic evaluation of the administrative performance of the Executive Branch. In the rhythm of congressional operations, two events occur which provide committees an opportunity to review program accomplishments. The first is when legislation is due to expire; at this point, as the authorizing committee considers whether to extend a program, it conducts hearings and occasionally commissions studies to assess the program's results and any needed changes in the law. The other is during the annual appropriations process, when the appropriations subcommittees of the House and Senate examine program operations.

The two authorizing committees for the Emergency Employment Act were Labor and Public Welfare in the Senate and Education and Labor in the House, but since this was a temporary program, authorized for only two years, they would not necessarily be considering proposals for extension. As it turned out, bills were introduced in 1972 and 1973 to extend and even expand the program. But the Nixon administration was adamantly against extension, and the lack of program advocacy from the Executive Branch reduced the opportunity for oversight hearings.

But as we saw earlier, the Senate Subcommittee on Employment, Manpower and Poverty had long been a strong proponent of public-service employment, so its chairman, Senator Gaylord Nelson, and its staff decided to keep a close watch on the Public Employment Program. To achieve this, Senator Nelson on July 28, 1971, wrote to Controller General Elmer B. Staats asking the General Accounting Office (GAO) to conduct an ongoing review and evaluation of the program.

Ten years earlier this request would have been foreign to the usual practices of GAO, which is fundamentally an accounting agency. However, in 1967 Senator Joseph Clark was able to gain Senator Winston Prouty's support for emergency employment by agreeing to a provision requiring the GAO to make an evaluation of programs of the Economic Opportunity Act. The emergency-employment amendment was defeated on the Senate floor, but Prouty's GAO amendment was adopted. This put GAO into program evaluation for the first time, and since then other legislation has called upon the GAO for program studies.

The first GAO report on emergency employment dealt with the issue of the allocation formula for Section 5 funds, and the controller general found nothing illegal about the Labor Department's two-part formula. The second report reviewed the speed of hiring during the first four months of the program. This was followed by four reports, spaced over eighteen months, on how a sample of twenty-five program agents (seven states, eight counties, and ten cities) carried out four important aspects of the program: planning, selection of participants, types of jobs offered, and public service benefits. Yet another report dealt with the Indian program. GAO published its reports and sent them to both the Senate and House labor committees and made them available to other members of Congress, the Executive Branch, and the interested public.[10]

The appropriations committees got their opportunity to review the Public Employment Program in the course of considering the Labor Department's request for the second year's funding. At a hearing on the House side,[11] Subcommittee Chairman Daniel J. Flood of Pennsylvania immediately brought up the issue of cities laying off people and then hiring them back. Secretary of Labor Hodgson said that, although this was not a widespread practice, the thirty-day requirement was necessary to prevent abuses. Assistant Secretary Lovell reported that 12 percent of all participants were former employees of the employing local agency. Flood and other members asked specific questions about other aspects of the program: the formula, maximum salary, length of employment, auditing, participation by veterans and public-assistance recipients, terminations and finding permanent jobs, average cost per enrollee, administrative costs, geographic breakdown of funds, allocation to small communities. The inquiry stressed fact-finding, not criticism, and there were no questions based upon research or massive complaints. One member asked, what have the major problems been? Manpower Administrator Paul J. Fasser, Jr., replied:

> Most of the problems encountered have concerned eligibility of the applicants. These dealt mainly with unmet residency requirements and the lack of a period of unemployment before entering the program. There were also some accounting problems. However, most of the problems were minor, and in view of the newness of the program it is premature to identify any problem as widespread or persistent at this time.[12]

As Representative Flood summarized the situation: "A little abuse here and there, but certainly no widespread abuse, no scandal—is that it?" Answered Secretary Hodgson: "If there is one thing surprising to me, it is there hasn't been more of that and more complaints about it."[13]

On the other side of Capitol Hill, Senators Warren G. Magnuson of Washington and Norris Cotton of New Hampshire conducted the hearing.[14] They wanted to know about numbers of enrollees and wages, manpower training and services, administrative costs, distribution of Section 6 funds, fringe benefits, substitution of federal for local funds, and demonstration projects. Senator Cotton asked how many "wardheelers" had been hired for political jobs. William Mirengoff, director of the Office of Public Service Employment, estimated that it would be much less than 1 percent. When Mirengoff boasted how fast the department had moved in getting the program underway, Senator Magnuson remarked:

> I think you would agree with me that a great deal of credit has to be given to the cities and the counties, and the States that had their programs all ready to go, anticipating the bill, and they did a good job in many cases.

Responded Mirengoff:

> Yes, sir. I remember Governors running around with messages and Mayors running Xerox machines and working weekends. It was a remarkable effort by the local governments.[15]

In this friendly atmosphere, both appropriation committees and the House of Representatives and the Senate voted the full appropriations for the second year of the Public Employment Program.

Outside Evaluation

Outside the federal government, several other studies of the Public Employment Program were undertaken. One of these was made by the National Manpower Policy Task Force, with financial support from a Ford Foundation grant. The Task Force is a private nonprofit organization of academicians who are specialists in manpower programs and policies. This particular study was directed by Sar A. Levitan, Task Force vice-chairman, and Robert Taggart, executive director. They commissioned seventeen scholars, most of them university-based, to undertake case histories of state and local program agents in their locales. In May, 1972, the Senate Subcommittee on Employment, Manpower and Poverty published an interim assessment by Levitan and Taggart and nine case studies of the first several months of operations by four states, nine cities, and one council of government.[16] A few months later the Task Force released a second interim report.[17] During 1973 the Subcommittee published Levitan and Taggart's evaluation of the first eighteen months of the emergency-employment program[18] and sixteen case studies.[19] An abridgment of the case studies was also prepared for publication by a commercial publisher.[20]

A second outside evaluation was undertaken by the National Urban Coalition. To supplement data obtained from the Labor Department, this study used twenty-two local urban coalitions to collect information on the twenty-six program agents functioning in their areas. The executive committee of the coalition reviewed the study's findings and recommendations and released the report in September, 1972.[21]

But nothing about what the evaluations said

12

PARTICIPANTS
AND THEIR JOBS

The political debate which preceded enactment of the Emergency Employment Act had a lot to say about whom the program would serve and what kinds of jobs they would fill. Now, experience had replaced supposition. By the end of June, 1973,* after the program had been operating nearly two years, 318,000 persons had held jobs under the Public Employment Program, including 13,000 youth hired for summer jobs in 1972.[1] Who were these people and what work did they perform?

Characteristics of Participants

As we saw in chapter one, national commissions advocating public-service employment during the 1960s favored jobs for the special clienteles which were the commissions' primary concern: hardcore unemployed, youth, rural residents, inhabitants of urban ghettoes, welfare recipients, etc. The most serious legislative effort was an attempt made in the Senate in 1967 to provide "emergency employment" aimed primarily at disadvantaged persons.

The rise in national unemployment which began in 1970 meant that increasing numbers of previously stable workers were without jobs. Declines in aerospace and defense industries put engineers and

---

*Data for this date are used because in the summer of 1973 a large number of youth were enrolled, distorting the statistical averages for subsequent cumulative enrollment.

technicians out of work, and winding down the war in Vietnam added many veterans to the ranks of the unemployed. This broader base of concern produced a congressional majority in favor of emergency employment and, six months after a presidential veto of such legislation, converted President Nixon and his White House advisers.

The Emergency Employment Act clearly stated that it was aimed at unemployed and underemployed persons. In its regulations, the Labor Department defined "unemployed" as being without work for seven days or longer, and "underemployed" as working only part-time while desiring full-time work or working full-time for wages producing family income below the poverty level.

In practice, though, program agents did not strictly adhere to the regulations. Interviewers from Westat, Inc., talked to a scientific sample of program participants, probing into their previous employment status, and found that quite a few had been employed the day before taking the PEP job. Westat reported that "the conclusion is inescapable that about a fifth of all PEP participants were not, strictly speaking, eligible. It also seems clear that those who were working immediately before enrollment regarded PEP jobs as more attractive than those they occupied at the time they sought to enroll in the program."[2]

As to specific participation, the Emergency Employment Act described diverse groups affected by unemployment, namely: low-income persons and migrants, persons of limited English-speaking ability, individuals from socioeconomic backgrounds generally associated with substantial unemployment and underemployment, young persons entering the labor force, persons who had recently been separated from military service, older persons who desired to remain in, enter, or reenter the labor force, welfare recipients, persons who had become unemployed or underemployed as a result of technological changes or as a result of shifts in the pattern of federal expenditures, as in the defense, aerospace, and construction industries.

Having referred to all these groups, the act required that an application for financial assistance should contain "a plan for effectively serving on an equitable basis the significant segments of the population to be served." Furthermore, there would have to be assurances that special consideration would be given to veterans who had served in Indochina or Korea after August 5, 1964, and due consideration would also be given to persons who had participated in manpower training and for whom other jobs were not immediately available. The Labor Department's guidelines paraphrased the act's requirements and set a goal whereby at least a third of all participants would be veterans who had served in the armed forces on or after August 5, 1964. This goal was raised to 40 percent the second year. (Note, though, that Indochina or Korean service was not mentioned in the guidelines.)

One way to test whether the Public Employment Program provided equitable participation of segments of the unemployed population is to compare characteristics of PEP participants with the unemployed generally. This is done in Table IV. Judging on this basis, we find that younger and older persons were underrepresented in the program. In the year-round program, older workers fared better than younger ones, but youth were hired for summer jobs for youth in 1972 and again in 1973. Throughout, persons aged twenty-two to forty-four were overrepresented compared to total unemployment.

Men have constituted 72 percent of PEP participants, compared to 54 percent of all unemployed.

Vietnam-era veterans have made up 29 percent of PEP enrollment, considerably more than their 7 percent in total national unemployment, but less than the one-third (later raised to 40 percent) goal established by the Labor Department. However, adding veterans with earlier service reaches over 43 percent of participation in PEP, compared to 17 percent veterans unemployment among all who were out of work.

The Public Employment Program served proportionately fewer persons who did not complete high school than this segment represents among all the unemployed, and more persons who had been to college. The high proportion of persons with high-school education and beyond and the preponderance of men aged twenty-two to forty-four suggest that the cream of the crop was selected much more frequently than the hard-core unemployed.

TABLE IV

Characteristics of Participants in Regulation Public-Employment Program Compared to Total U. S. Unemployment, August, 1971 to June, 1973*

Characteristic	Emergency Employment August 1971 to June 1973 (percentages)	U. S. Unemployment Composite average (percentages)
Age		
21 and less	19	36
22 to 44	66	43
45 and over	14	21
Sex		
Male	72	54
Female	28	46
Military Service		
Vietnam-era Veterans	29	7
Other Veterans	14	10
Nonveterans	57	83
Education (highest grade completed)		
Less than 12	26	42
12	43	40
13 and more	31	18
Weeks Unemployed (current spell)		
4 and less	24	47
5 to 14	23	30
15 and more	52	23
Racial/Ethnic Group		
White	60	77
Black	24 ⎫	⎫
Oriental	1 ⎬ 27	⎬ 18
American-Indian	2 ⎭	⎭
Spanish-American	13	5

*Excludes summer youth program
Source: Manpower Administration, Agent Information System

But the program reached more long-term unemployed than this group represents in total unemployment, and also proportionately more blacks and Spanish-Americans. Program agents classified 38 percent of the participants as "disadvantaged," but a number of evaluators have concluded that too many nondisadvantaged minority persons were put into that category. Data produced by Westat, Inc., suggest that 18 percent is a more accurate figure for disadvantaged participants, slightly above the 16 to 17 percent this group represents in total unemployment.[3]

In a study released in September, 1972, the National Urban Coalition commended the program for its successful efforts to involve minority groups but criticized the relatively low participation of persons with less than a high-school education. Local urban coalitions reported that program agents "generally hired the conventionally desirable participants and accommodated whatever others were necessary to satisfy the Labor Department's minimum guidelines."[4]

The General Accounting Office, in its examination of twenty-five program agents, found that only eleven achieved the first-year goal of one-third hiring of Vietnam-era veterans. Because of lack of local data, GAO could not determine whether various groups of unemployed persons, such as young or disadvantaged persons, were being properly represented among those being hired by the program agents surveyed, but it did find that the applicants hired were usually those deemed the best qualified.[5]

A number of the case studies produced for the National Manpower Policy Task Force suggested that there was significant "creaming" within every category of unemployed. For instance, three-fifths of those classified as "disadvantaged" had a high-school diploma and a number had some college education. Analyzing these studies and national data, Levitan and Taggart observed:

In all likelihood, then, PEP could have had more impact on unemployment if it had hired more participants with limited qualifications who were actively seeking but unable to find jobs. Fewer college graduates and more high school dropouts would have meant more people otherwise unemployed and a faster filtering down of extra jobs to those most in need. An increased percentage of women already looking for work as opposed to wives previously outside the labor force (25 percent of all female participants) would have magnified the impact.

Without arguing on equity grounds, it thus would have made more sense to direct PEP to a more disadvantaged clientele. More persons could have been hired, and the unemployment reducing impact of this hiring would probably have been greater.[6]

But the political facts of life, both nationally and locally, focused on neither social equity nor maximum economic impact. As the National Urban Coalition pointed out, the "emergency" was not that of disadvantaged groups, which had long experienced substantial unemployment, but rather a high national unemployment rate which hit many more people.[7]

Three other categories of participants deserve mention. Nine percent were former enrollees in federal manpower-training programs, a group the Emergency Employment Act required be given due consideration. Ten percent had been previously employed by the program agent, subagent, or employing agent and had been rehired after the thirty-day waiting period—at first a troublesome issue in a few places, but not everywhere. And only 5 percent were classified as professionals, plus 3 percent as teachers, although the act permitted up to a third professionals, not including teachers.

Wages

The restriction on hiring professionals had been added by the House of Representatives, along with a salary ceiling of $12,000 paid by federal funds. Through June, 1973, the average wage was $2.88 an hour, which the Labor Department computed to be equivalent to $5,921 for a full year's work. Participants also received an average of $772 in fringe benefits on an annualized basis, making a total of $6,693 per man-year in wages and benefits. Other direct costs included $145 per man-year for training, $60 for supportive services, $850 for local administration, and $112 for federal administration. This amounted to a total cost of $7,860 per man-year, of which federal funds paid for seven-eighths.

On the average, participants remained in PEP jobs for forty-one weeks. This means that the average participant cost was about $6,200, including training, supportive services, and administrative expenses.

On the average, PEP participants had received $2.77 an hour in the last job held before entering the program, so that the average wage of $2.88 represented a slight advance. Breaking this down by major occupational groups reveals, however, that for some persons PEP wages were lower than those earned on previous jobs, while for other persons they were higher. Specifically, wages were up for clerical, sales, service, bench work, farming, and forestry occupations, and down for professional, technical, managerial, processing, machine trades, and structural work. Thus, in wages paid PEP was something of a "leveler."

The Jobs

The kinds of jobs which might be provided through public-service employment drew lots of attention during the political debate which preceded enactment of the legislation. President Nixon, in his December, 1970, veto message, spoke out against "dead-end jobs in the public sector." On the Senate floor, Peter Dominick said it would be "make-work." Proponents countered with studies made by municipal associations and the National Urban Coalition showing that a wide variety of unmet public needs could absorb hundreds of thousands of new workers.

As it turned out, the program agents and subagents had no great difficulty in finding useful work to be done. Though enrollment did not go as fast as the Labor Department wanted, 89,000 persons were working by December 31, 1971. This number nearly doubled in the next six months, reaching a peak of 185,000 in July, 1972 (including 12,000 in a special summer youth program). By then all funds were committed (in fact, overcommitted) and a freeze was put into effect. The early delays in hiring were due to civil-service restrictions, court suits, union objections, and management shortcomings, not lack of work to be done.

The public-service areas in which the work was performed are shown in Table V. Public works and transportation (streets and highways) took the greatest number of workers, and many of these jobs were for unskilled and semiskilled labor. Education was a close second, with both teaching and subprofessional jobs. Law enforcement, parks and recreation, and health and hospitals were grouped in the next rank.

TABLE V

Public-Service Areas of Public-Employment Program Jobs, August, 1971, to June, 1973

Public-Service Area	Percent Unemployment
Public works and transportation	22
Education	20
Law enforcement	11
Health and hospitals	9
Parks and recreation	8
Social service	6
Environmental quality	4
Fire protection	2
Administrative and other	17

Source: Manpower Administration, Agent Information System

Levitan and Taggart compared this distribution of jobs with regular public employment and found two major discrepancies. Public works and transportation accounted for only 7 percent of state and local employment in 1971 but 22 percent of PEP jobs during the first twenty months of the program. And whereas slightly over half the state and local public jobs are in education, this area was assigned only 20 percent of the PEP participants. This was due in part to the fact that city, county, and state governments, not school districts, were the program agents, and the officials of general government were inclined to assign jobs to their own departments. Levitan and Taggart further explain that, in distributing jobs, "mayors, governors, and county executives were justifiably uncertain about the future of PEP, and they wanted jobs which could be started and then stopped without any permanent commitments." This would be easier in public works, streets and highways, and parks and recreation, where a lot of short-term projects could be carried out, and harder in education and health care, which are more institutionalized and cannot handle temporary employment as easily.[8]

Commenting on the occupations filled by the Public Employment Program, Levitan and Taggart remark:

> Not surprisingly, PEP jobs are similar to those already being carried out at the state and local level. Broken down by detailed occupations, and stripped of the assorted titles which give the appearance of innovative new careeers, most of the jobs are familiar —i.e., clerks, typists, guards, maintenance men, road crews, repairmen, warehousemen, and a few teachers and administrators.
>
> Whether or not the PEP jobs are "make-work" depends upon individual evaluation of the work performed. It is clear, however, that in most cases equipment and personnel have been marshalled to utilize the new workers, functions are being performed, and employers are apparently satisfied with the output. Most program agents have asked for more PEP funds.[9]

The *Manpower Report of the President: 1975,* reflecting upon PEP experience, made the following observation about the jobs undertaken:

> Perhaps the best criteria for judging the usefulness of the positions created under PEP are the feelings of the workers and supervisors involved in the program. Reports from both regular and high-impact programs indicated that most employees felt their jobs were fulfilling public service needs. In addition, most supervisors indicated a high level of satisfaction with their PEP employees, ranking them as generally better than average in their work habits and efficiency when compared with regular government employees.[10]

Public Service Benefits

One purpose of the Emergency Employment Act was to fill unmet service needs. The General Accounting Office explored whether this objective was being achieved by a sample of nine program agents and found that it was. According to the GAO:

> The majority of the program agents contacted said using EEA participants helped to meet public service needs and they were pleased with the participants' on-the-job performance. Although many agencies used EEA participants to establish new services, officials of the employing agencies said the primary benefit from employing EEA participants was the improvement of existing services. In several locations EEA funds were used to provide jobs to restore or continue services eliminated or cut back because of budgetary problems.
>
> In a related review involving six other program agents operating public employment programs in rural and urban areas, we found that in the urban areas the program generally served to prevent a decrease in city services rather than to provide additional services and that in the rural areas the program generally served to provide additional needed services.[11]

And the Executive Branch reached similar conclusions about the value of public services provided through the Public Employment Program. The *Manpower Report of the President: 1975* pointed out:

> When PEP was enacted, there were fears that many of the jobs would be "make work" or that some of the rapidly hired new workers would lack the equipment or supervision needed to perform productive public services. Although there may have been some misallocation or inefficiency during the rapid startup phase, later evaluations underscored the fact that most of the jobs created were providing useful public services.[12]

Section 6: Special Employment Assistance

When the emergency-employment legislation was before the House Education and Labor Committee, Representative Carl Perkins wanted a provision to send additional funds to areas of chronically high unemployment, such as Eastern Kentucky, and Representative Augustus Hawkins had a similar concern for high-unemployment areas within cities, such as South Central Los Angeles.

Section 6 was the result, and it authorized $250 million during each year of the program for assistance to such areas.

Where an entire county or city qualified for Section 6 funds, the money was in effect combined with the Section 5 grant and the two were run as a single program. Where special areas were demarcated within cities and counties, the Section 6 component had to retain separate identity for purposes of recruitment and possibly for selection of work sites.

National statistics produced by the Manpower Administration reveal no major differences between participants and jobs in the Section 5 and Section 6 programs. But the man-year cost for Section 6 was slightly lower, partly because the Emergency Employment Act did not authorize training and support services under Section 6, and partly because persons filling the higher-paid jobs in cities are less likely to live in neighborhoods with high unemployment.

After the National Urban Coalition protested that the lack of training funds for Section 6 made it harder for program agents to recruit disadvantaged persons in high-unemployment neighborhoods, the Labor Department issued a memorandum to the field giving program agents permission to use Section 5 money to provide training and supportive services to Section 6 participants. But the coalition's study concluded that the memorandum had little effect.

The Labor Department's Section 6 guidelines specified that, wherever possible, the jobs provided and the services rendered should be within designated areas. Nevertheless, in the cities studied by the National Urban Coalition

no effort was made, nor any system established, to introduce an area emphasis for Section 6 programs, where the entire city or county had a high unemployment rate above 6 percent. Nor is there any indication that attempts were made to recruit area residents for jobs that would serve unmet public service needs in their own neighborhoods.[13]

Demonstration Projects

The two demonstration programs provided additional jobs in two dozen localities, but as social experiments they drifted away from the models originally propounded, the welfare demonstration more so than the high-impact demonstration.

The initial concept of the high-impact demonstration contemplated sufficient funding to provide nine areas with enough money to hire 10 percent of the unemployed, and three areas with enough funds to hire 15 percent of the unemployed in the first year and 25 percent in the second. The intended second-year increase never occurred in these three areas, but nevertheless one area had produced jobs for 28.1 percent of its unemployed, while the other two areas of the second model employed 10.6 percent and 13.7 percent in PEP jobs. In the other nine areas an average of 6.8 percent of the unemployed gained work through PEP.[14] Since these jobs amounted to only 1 or 2 percent of the total labor force, they had virtually no influence on the overall wage level.[15]

These PEP jobs ranged from 1.2 percent to 8.2 percent of regular employment of state and local government in the areas. In its evaluation study, the National Planning Association (NPA) determined that "no serious absorption problems were encountered."[16] Plenty of public-service jobs were easily found. The most dramatic case was Woodruff, South Carolina (population 4,600), which increased city personnel from fifteen to fifty-two with notable impact through increased public services. Apparently it would take much higher saturation of public-service employment to exhaust the number of job opportunities or affect private wages.

However, NPA concluded that the localities substituted some of the PEP jobs for jobs which would have been otherwise created through normal expansion of governmental jobs. Using microeconometric methods to compare these localities with matched localities, NPA indicated that only 54 percent of the PEP jobs were positions which would not otherwise have existed.[17]

As to economic impact, the unemployment level in the high-impact areas decreased somewhat more than could have been expected had the program not existed, but the NPA study was not able to establish any clear relationship between the sizes of decrease in each area and the relative number of PEP jobs. Neither were there any measurable effects on total employment or income levels.[18]

"Participants received substantial increases in earnings during and after PEP as compared with what they could have expected in the absence of the program," NPA reported.[19] This was similar to the Public Employment Program as a whole, and there were other similarities. Characteristics of participants, types of work performed, and transition into permanent jobs were not markedly different. Program administration was handled by the same agencies, which absorbed this additional assignment without undue difficulties. In short, the high-impact projects represented merely an enlargement of the regular Section 5 program.

The welfare demonstration was another matter, for it encountered many delays. By its nature it was administered by another network of agencies: a different office in the Labor Department, a unit in the Department of Health, Education and Welfare, state employment services, and state and county welfare departments. These agencies took quite a while to work out the necessary relationships—much longer than the high-impact demonstration—but eventually the administrative difficulties were overcome.

The experimental design had to be altered because the models for high and low support did not fit the localities to which the federal agencies assigned them. In the summer of 1972, Congress passed the Talmadge amendment to the welfare program, which made registration for employment or training mandatory for all employable welfare recipients. In a sense, this ended the opportunity to have some localities observe a voluntary model, but in practice the amendment had little effect because there were far more work applicants than the 6,000 available demonstration jobs. So it was the mandatory aspect which was never tested. In the end, no clear distinctions could be made between models utilized by the twelve participating localities.[20]

As might have been expected, most participants were women and most of the jobs were in health, social services, and education. With so few jobs, the demonstration could have little success in reducing the welfare rolls, but it showed that many on welfare would work if offered the opportunity.

Transition to other jobs proved to be more difficult in the welfare demonstration than in the regular PEP program (described in the next chapter). As of April, 1974, when Decision Making Information (DMI) conducted its third and final wave of interviews, 22 percent of the participants were still working at PEP jobs, 38 percent were otherwise employed, and 40 percent were not working. Of those employed in non-PEP jobs, 18 percent (of total enrollment) were holding project jobs which had become permanent, 7 percent were working for public agencies in other kinds of jobs, 11 percent were in private employment, and 2 percent were self-employed. Of those not working, 20 percent were seeking work and 20 percent had dropped out of the labor market.[21]

Nevertheless, DMI concluded in its final evaluation report that a fundamental goal was achieved because the experience of the demonstration "indicates that public service employment for welfare recipients is a viable alternative to income maintenance."[22]

13

TRANSITIONAL
EMPLOYMENT

As related in chapters two and three, providing transition to permanent jobs was a major issue in the legislative debate leading to enactment of the Emergency Employment Act. The absence of such provisions was one reason President Nixon used for vetoing the bill in December, 1970. Republicans brought up the issue repeatedly during the legislative process in the spring of 1971, and as noted earlier, Congress larded the final version of the act with frequent references to transitional employment.

With this background, the Labor Department's guidelines contained a strong statement on transitional employment:

> The goal of the Act is to place unemployed and underemployed persons in transitional jobs which will enable individuals to move into permanent employment in the public or private sector. To achieve this goal, special consideration must be given to jobs which provide prospects for non-subsidized employment with the employment agency or other employer. The Program Agent's plans should provide for needed training and related manpower services to promote the movement of participants to regular employment or training and to provide participants with skills for which there is an anticipated high demand.
>
> Program Agents and the employing agencies responsible to them must plan to place at least half of the EEA participants in continuing positions with the Program Agent or the employing agencies which are financed by non-EEA funds.[1]

Faced with this requirement, the program agents did indeed pledge to achieve the goal of 50 percent placement in regular public jobs. But as the program progressed neither the Department of Labor nor most program agents gave much attention to the matter. Nevertheless, by September, 1972, when the program had been going over a year, 31 percent of the participants had moved to permanent jobs in the public sector.[2]

Field interviews conducted in the spring and early summer of 1972 in several localities by staff from the Center for Governmental Studies (Washington, D. C.) found that program agents were not giving this objective much thought because they were under no particular pressure from the Labor Department to do so. Since it was a two-year program, they felt no urgency to transfer participants to jobs on the regular payroll. Some of them had earmarked funds in next year's budget for this purpose, but they were in no hurry to use local funds as long as they could keep people employed with federal funds.

Then in July, 1972, the Labor Department instituted a job freeze during which there was no new hiring and no refilling of jobs vacated by participants leaving the program. This occurred because Congress had not yet approved the PEP appropriation for the 1973 fiscal year and had passed instead a continuing resolution to keep the program going at its present level of $1 billion until final action could be taken on the appropriations request of $1.25 billion for the new fiscal year. Furthermore, the inevitable lag in hiring at the start of the program meant that program agents had built up a surplus of funds, which many had used to create more jobs than originally envisioned. Now the Labor Department wanted them to reduce enrollment to a level which could be financed on a twelve-month basis.

Since this meant that any time an employing agency placed a participant into a permanent position it would lose the PEP job vacated, it was a disincentive to the transitional process. The hiring freeze was lifted in September for program agents which had never used all authorized positions and accordingly had funds to bring their programs to that level, but this was no help to the vigorous programs which had filled all their jobs. Then in October, the

President vetoed the appropriations bill for the Department of Labor and Health, Education and Welfare, and Congress kept the continuing resolution in force. This cast further doubt on the future of PEP. And when the President's budget came out in January, 1973, with an announcement that he intended to phase out PEP, the program agents, with the freeze still on, gained an even stronger incentive to hold on to jobs for as long as possible.

Throughout this period of funding uncertainty, the Labor Department gave program agents funding extensions on a month-to-month basis with position authorization based on first-year funding levels. Where the jobs were not filled, the uncommitted funds went back to the national fund to be allocated during the phase-out period. This meant that every time a participant left the program, the locality would lose funds. Thus, the funding arrangements during the second year worked against the transition process.

By way of illustration, in the two-month period of May and June, 1972, when the national unemployment rate averaged 5.7 percent, program agents recruited 46,000 new participants and terminated 26,000. Six months later in November and December, when unemployment was down to 5.3 percent, they added 9,000 enrollees and terminated 17,000 for a net decrease of 8,000. In other words, the program agents had earlier demonstrated their ability to use PEP for transitional employment, but they pursued this course with less enthusiasm, even with a brighter employment picture, because of reduced incentives.

Results

In spite of this lack of incentives, participants moved through the program into other jobs with considerable regularity. Westat, Inc. followed its scientific sample of participants through June, 1974, three years after the program began, and found that 90 percent who had participated had moved on to something else. Those who had terminated had spent an average of 13.2 months in PEP. Women, who constituted slightly less than a fourth of the enrollment, stayed in the program slightly longer than men. Older persons were enrolled longer than younger ones; for example, those eighteen to twenty-one held PEP jobs an average of 13.0 months compared to 14.6 months for persons forty-five and older. Disadvantaged persons did not stay on quite as long as the nondisadvantaged.[3]

Employment status of terminees is shown in Table VI. One month after leaving PEP, over three-fourths were employed, and that percentage rose above 80 in subsequent months. At the same time, unemployment dropped from 12 percent to 5.8 percent eighteen months after leaving PEP but rose to 8 percent twenty-four months after. (National unemployment was fairly stable throughout this period, but was beginning to rise toward the end of the Westat survey.) Between 11 and 12 percent of the PEP terminees dropped out of the labor force in the months after they left PEP.[4]

TABLE VI

Distribution of Labor-Force Status of PEP Terminees at Selected Time Periods

Time Period	% Employed	% Unemployed	% Not in Labor Force
1 month post-PEP	76.4	11.9	11.7
6 months post-PEP	81.2	7.9	11.0
12 months post-PEP	82.2	6.6	11.2
24 months post-PEP	80.9	8.0	11.1

Source: Westat, Inc., *Longitudinal Evaluation of the Public Employment Program and Validation of the PEP Data Bank.* Final Report, pp. 6-24.

Of those employed, 65.2 percent worked for public employers six months after leaving PEP. This percentage dropped to 57.2 percent after twelve months, 53.8 percent at eighteen months, and 46.8 percent at twenty-four months. Thus, initially, a little over half of all terminees (including those not in the labor force) remained in some kind of public employment, indicating that, on the average, program agents met the goal of 50 percent transition to public sector jobs.[5]

The same survey by Westat revealed that the average wage of those employed one month after leaving the Public Employment

Program was $3.45 per hour. This compared to an average of $2.82 an hour earned by PEP participants who were working six months before entering the program (53 percent were so employed).[6]

Westat also calculated before and after annualized earning rates. On the average, PEP participants earned $3,184 a year before PEP and $5,609 a year after, a 76 percent increase.[7] White participants averaged $3,079 a year before and $5,835 after; blacks $2,535 before and $4,911 after; and Spanish-Americans $2,347 before and $6,058 after.[8] Thus, since $4,275 was the poverty line for a family of four in 1972, PEP and post-PEP employment served as an antipoverty device for many persons.

On the basis of data gathered in four waves of interviews with PEP participants and terminees, Westat concluded:

> For the average participant, having a job in the Public Employment Program was of assistance in obtaining unsubsidized employment. In fact, two-thirds of all terminees responding at Wave IV (not only those working but those unemployed or out of the labor force as well) considered their PEP experience to have been helpful in finding post-program employment.

> The data support their view. By any measures we chose—labor force participant rates, unemployment rates, hourly wages, annualized earnings, dependency on publicly-funded programs— PEP participants in general were better off after enrolling than they were before and the concept of "transitional employment" as embodied in the Act, in the Regulations and in guidance to Program Agents proved successful.[9]

Training and Manpower Services

President Nixon, in his veto message of December, 1970, and Secretary of Labor Hodgson, in his March, 1971, testimony to the House subcommittee, both stressed the importance of skill training as a means of preparing participants for unsubsidized jobs. The Nelson and Daniels bills made training a permissible activity, and the final version of the Emergency Employment Act allowed up to 15 percent of Section 5 funds to be used for training and manpower services.

Nevertheless, all concerned saw PEP as basically a jobs program and recognized that training programs under other manpower legislation could be utilized by PEP participants. This was emphasized by the statutory requirement that at least 85 percent of the funds go for participants' wages and employment benefits. After the House Appropriations Committee underscored this point by reducing the budget for administration, the Labor Department issued guidelines requiring that 90 percent of the Section 5 funds and 96.8 percent of Section 6 funds be used for wages and fringe benefits. Not more than 3.2 percent from the two sections could go for administrative expenses of program agents. This left 6.8 percent of Section 5 money which could either be used for training and supportive services or added to the wages-and-fringe-benefits account. Most program agents took the latter course and used less than 1 percent of their federal funds for training and supportive services.

The federal guidelines, while acknowledging the importance of training for upward mobility, also recognized the limited amount of emergency-employment funds for this purpose. So the Labor Department referred program agents to other federally assisted manpower programs. It was up to each program agent to work out its own arrangements. Some did, and on the average one-sixth of program agents' share of cost went for training and supportive services.

One that did was San Antonio, Texas, where PEP was run by the Personnel Department, which also was responsible for the Public Service Careers program (PSC). The PSC director, who played a leading role in writing the emergency-employment application, retained a strong interest in training programs and accordingly arranged for many PEP participants to receive training under Public Service Careers. This bolstered their chances to gain permanent status under civil service.[10]

Wichita, Kansas, also used the PSC program to train participants in the Public Employment Program. In addition, the city used PEP funds for courses at the area vocational technical school and at universities. Washington, D.C., did the same through Federal City College, a technical institute, and the Opportunities Industrialization Center (OIC). The district government referred participants to a PSC program in basic education and clerical skills, and it offered a course in skills needed to pass federal civil-service examinations.[11]

Transition Techniques

In their evaluation of the first eighteen months of PEP, Levitan and Taggart concluded that, without training, transition is a revolving door.[12] However, Everett Crawford in a study of transitional employment, while endorsing the need for training, identified four other approaches to encouraging transition into regular public jobs.[13]

The first approach is to pay attention to anticipated *attrition and turnover* in public employment. In Seattle, the city's manpower staff, with assistance from the Budget Office and the Personnel Department, conducted a survey of the city's entire personnel complement and found that many employees were reaching retirement age. About eighty-five firemen were expected to retire within two years, and so were a number of drivers in the transit system. There was a high turnover in clerical and stenographic positions and among teachers and other school personnel and, furthermore, expansion of school enrollment was projected. Therefore, approximately a hundred firemen-trainee positions were created, and within a year sixty had transferred to the regular force. About sixty drivers were hired under PEP; half of them were taken on as regulars within a year, and prospects were good for the remainder. However, turnover in school and clerical positions was not as high as expected, and school enrollment did not expand as much as predicted (because of high unemployment in Seattle, many persons were not leaving jobs or moving to the area). Some teachers and some clerical personnel did experience transition, but not as many as expected.

Some states and cities used *new approaches to civil service*. In Massachusetts, the Department of Manpower Affairs worked out an arrangement to make PEP positions exempt from civil-service procedures so that hiring could occur without an entrance examination. Then the legislature passed an amendment to permit entry-level appointments into civil service without a competitive examination for persons who had participated in federal manpower programs, including PEP. However, such persons would have to take a noncompetitive qualifying test, and they would have to compete for future promotions. A similar arrangement was utilized in Philadelphia through adaptation of a system already in use for personnel working in the model-cities program. Participants could be appointed without a competitive exam, and if their performance was satisfactory after six months they could take a qualifying examination and gain a provisional appointment while remaining on the emergency-employment payroll. Later they could transfer to a regular civil-service job when vacancies occurred and budgets permitted.

New positions were created on an experimental basis with PEP funds, with the intention of making them into regular jobs if they proved of value. The county hospital in Dauphin County, Pennsylvania (Harrisburg is the county's principal city) established positions for medical assistants and patient advocates. The medical assistant has more training than a registered nurse but less than a physician, and the patient advocate helps patients get needed services and answers to their questions. Both positions proved to be assets to the hospital and were made permanent jobs.

An idea of using emergency employment as a *manpower pool* was beginning to develop when the Labor Department instituted the position freeze in the summer of 1972. Since governmental units have as difficult a time as other employers in securing good personnel when labor markets are tight, a pool of subsidized employees could be developed and drawn upon as regular jobs opened up. Such a system would be especially useful in helping disadvantaged persons acquire skills and job experience. Both King County, Washington, and its largest city, Seattle, had preliminary plans to organize such manpower pools, the city through its personnel department to serve municipal agencies, and the county through a computerized system which county agencies, municipalities outside Seattle, and school districts could call upon. But the plans were sidetracked when Washington clamped a lid on the Public Employment Program.

Transition to Private Sector Jobs

On a national basis, 65 percent of employed PEP terminees were working in public jobs six months after leaving PEP, and 47 percent had such jobs two years after termination, even though only 16 percent of the civilian labor force held government jobs. This preference for regular public employment rather than private jobs was partly due to the emphasis on this kind of transition in the federal guidelines and partly because of the ease in transferring to regular positions with the agencies already employing them. It was also a result of less attention given by both the Labor Department and most program agents to the possibilities of private employment.

There were, however, some exceptions. Massachusetts undertook an intensive job-development effort, conducted by state personnel handling emergency employment and by subagents around the state. In Lowell, Massachusetts, the director of emergency employment was also coordinator of a semiannual "job fair" of private employers, and he made arrangements for program participants to be interviewed for private jobs on these occasions. Milwaukee worked with the state employment service, other employment agencies, and major industries to uncover private jobs.[14] Altogether about a third of those employed after leaving PEP were working for private employers six months later, and this increased to slightly over half by the end of twenty-four months.

14

NEW FEDERALISM

AND

INSTITUTIONAL CHANGE

Division of power within the federal system has long been a focus of public concern in the United States. *The Federalist Papers* (1787–88) are full of discussion of this topic, and national, regional, state. and local leaders have debated the issue ever since.

In responding to the economic crisis of prolonged depression. Franklin D. Roosevelt's New Deal expanded the role of the national government in domestic affairs, and Harry Truman's Fair Deal continued this course. Dwight D. Eisenhower's administration slowed but did not abate the trend. John F. Kennedy's New Frontier renewed the drive for fresh national programs, and Lyndon B. Johnson's Great Society reached new heights of initiative in Washington. But as he got into his first full term, President Johnson saw that merely increasing federal financial support was insufficient to solve domestic problems. Thus he began to talk about "creative federalism," which he explained in a memorandum to his cabinet as follows:

The basis of creative federalism is cooperation.

If Federal assistance programs to State and local governments are to achieve their goals, more is needed than money alone. Effective organization, management and administration are required at each level of government. These programs must be carried out jointly; therefore, they should be worked out and planned in a cooperative spirit with those chief officials of State and local governments who are answerable to their citizens.[1]

While Johnson emphasized partnership, President Nixon advocated devolution of power. In an address to the nation on domestic programs in August, 1969, he stated:

> After a third of a century of power flowing from the people and the States to Washington it is time for a New Federalism in which power, funds, and responsibility will flow from Washington to the States and to the people.[2]

But Nixon's advocacy of his New Federalism ran counter to the habit of a generation of congressional Democrats, that of enacting national legislation for each new problem which emerges as a public concern. In this spirit, Congress added public-service-employment features to the Employment and Manpower Act of 1970. Nixon countered with a veto, declaring that "such a program represents a reversion to the remedies that were tried thirty-five years ago. Surely it is an inappropriate and ineffective response to the problems of the seventies."[3]

Yet the following July, when President Nixon accepted this program as a political and economic necessity, he and his advisers saw it as an opportunity to implement concepts of the New Federalism. With the fervor of converts, White House staff pushed the Department of Labor to get the money out fast so unemployed persons could be quickly hired. This could occur only if the federal bureaucracy would forego many of its habitual guidelines and accustomed detailed review of grant applications. And this was accomplished.

From a federal-program perspective, this act was a modified form of revenue sharing. The money was not entirely unrestricted because it was targeted at a specific objective, i.e., the hiring of the unemployed, with preference given to certain segments of this population. But many programmatic details were left up to the states, cities, and counties. This approach proved effective as state and local governments moved quickly to identify jobs which needed doing and to recruit the unemployed. And they handled large sums of money with scarcely a taint of misuse.

From the viewpoint of economic policy, the Public Employment Program represented a countercyclical strategy, and a modestly successful one. As Sar Levitan and Robert Taggart have observed:

Possibly the most significant lesson is that a public employment program can be an effective countercyclical tool and that such a program deserves top consideration in a strategy to achieve an economy of high employment. The program dispelled any doubts about the timeliness of government action and the high impact experiments showed that the scale could be increased two to three times without losing much effectiveness. . . . There is strong evidence that PEP has more immediate job creation pay-off per dollar than any alternative government policy.[4]

But as the program continued, Labor Department bureaucrats began to reassert their old habits. Some zealous field representatives gave their personal interpretation of regulations, and as the months wore on regional offices took longer to review applications and requests to amend grant conditions. For example, job titles listed in program agents' proposals could not be changed without regional-office approval, and this involved action by several different units at a regional office. Guidelines from Washington grew longer and more detailed. The job freeze in the summer of 1972 increased federal controls.

Nevertheless, since state and local programs were shaped largely in the beginning months when local and state initiative was at its maximum, the Public Employment Program maintained greater local variation than any previous manpower program.

A major by-product was the strengthened capacity of state and local governments, particularly elected chief executives, to administer employment and manpower programs. Before, most manpower programs had been monopolized by established state agencies and local private nonprofit organizations. Grants to governors in 1969 and to 130 mayors in 1970 for hiring manpower planners gave most of these chief executives their first involvement in this program field, and more often than not it was this staff which prepared the original application for PEP funds (though they usually did not become the program administrators). And for most of the 368 counties which became program agents, this was the first time they had anything to do with a federally supported manpower program; and then in 1973 the large counties also began getting manpower-planning grants. Altogether, the experience so gained set the stage for further efforts to place more responsibility for manpower programs in the hands of local and state elected officials.

In addition to institutional development, the Public Employment Program produced changes in local and state practices (though not as much as some change advocates had hoped). In Congress, many of the proponents of a public-service employment program had a particular concern for disadvantaged persons—those who suffered a high rate of unemployment because of insufficient education, lack of occupational skills, or discriminatory employment practices. Consequently, the Emergency Employment Act listed such groups as intended participants, and to serve the disadvantaged better, the act called for civil-service reform, job restructuring, and linkages with training and supportive services provided by other manpower programs. But the act also specified veterans and the technologically displaced as eligible participants, and Congress did not appropriate nearly as much money as would be needed to serve all those eligible.

As chapter twelve related, blacks and Spanish-Americans fared well statistically in comparison to their proportion among the unemployed, but the ones who benefitted individually were generally the better educated and more occupationally experienced. And no wonder, because program agents felt no pressure from the Labor Department to do otherwise. This experience led Levitan and Taggart to conclude:

> Hands Off Means Business As Usual: Another lesson from PEP is that without carefully spelled out preferences among the unemployed, the clients generally served by manpower programs will be shortchanged. . . . Almost without fail, program agents have creamed from each client group to get the best educated and most skilled workers. There has been very little reaching back down the labor queue. If this is to be achieved, much more careful stipulations must be offered.[5]

Neither was there much push from the Labor Department for states, cities, and counties to carry out the institutional changes necessary to provide greater employment opportunities for the disadvantaged. Nevertheless, many program agents on their own initiative undertook special recruitment efforts, civil-service reforms, and creation of new types of jobs.

J. A. Reyes Associates examined the situation in twenty localities scattered around the nation and concluded that PEP's impact on hiring procedures occurred most frequently in three areas: (a) the creation of new lower-level jobs; (b) the easing of qualifications for existing jobs; and (c) the revision of existing examinations to increase their relevancy to job requirements—and the fairness of their application to various population subgroups.[6]

Specific examples of changes in these areas have been mentioned in earlier chapters: recruitment outposts in black neighborhoods of Winston-Salem; bypassing of normal testing procedures for firemen in Wilmington, Delaware; a priority system for ranking applicants by the Berkshire Manpower Commission; entry-level appointments without competitive examination in the Massachusetts civil service system; selective certification in San Diego; generic classification in Baltimore; bilingual teacher aides in the Chicago schools; new positions of medical assistant and patient advocate in the hospital run by Dauphin County, Pennsylvania; training of PEP participants tied to the Public Service Careers program in San Antonio in order to enhance transition to permanent jobs; and selection of jobs with expected vacancies due to retirement and customary turnover in Seattle.

Some of the momentum for these kinds of changes had been started by previous federal programs and federal requirements for affirmative action to provide equal opportunity, but most of the specific innovations were locally designed and initiated. The Public Employment Program gave local and state officials an opportunity to bring about kinds of institutional change already on their agendas.

In this manner, the hopes of the New Federalism bore fruit. Many mayors and city managers, county commissioners and officials from councils of governments, governors, and state and local department heads took hold of the Public Employment Program and molded it into an instrument suitable for local conditions. Even so, some of the fears of persons skeptical of the New Federalism were realized, for the widespread occurrence of "creaming" and the relative neglect of disadvantaged persons showed that the drive for greater equality of opportunity still needed the influential weight of the federal government behind it. On balance, though, the Public Employment Program achieved a workable compromise between local initiative and federal direction.

Nevertheless, ultimately it was a federal program, financed in Washington. When the Nixon administration decided the emergency was over, it moved to close down the program, while congressional Democrats, joined by some Republicans, tried to keep it alive. No matter how important local and state elected officials considered the program to be in their localities, the decision to extend the funding of emergency employment was not theirs to make. That is to say, New Federalism did not change the truth of the adage, who pays the piper calls the tune—or more accurately, decides whether the piper may continue to perform.

The importance of Washington decisions was vividly evident in the next round of public debate on employment policy—events which were an epilogue to the Emergency Employment Act of 1971 but a prologue to a larger Public Employment Program designed to cope with the deeper recession which afflicted the nation in 1974 and 1975. Clearly, public officials' perceptions of job creation through public employment were strongly influenced by the PEP experience. This can be illustrated by two quotations.

The Joint Economic Committee of Congress, under Democratic control, stated in March, 1974:

> Coming high unemployment rates dramatize the need for a public service employment program. The Emergency Employment Act of 1971 demonstrated the efficacy of a public service employment program. Public service programs can be activated with reasonable speed (100,000 jobs were filled in the first five months of the Emergency Employment Act) and have low administrative costs per job created (94 percent of the Federal funds were used for job creation, with less than 5 percent used for Federal and local administrative costs). The program's success in creating jobs per dollar spent cannot be matched by any other type of public expenditure. Thus the public service employment program can be an

effective countercyclical tool and is essential to any strategy to achieve high employment.

A permanent public service employment program should be available for activation whenever national unemployment rates exceed 4.5 percent for any 3 month period. It should be targeted at those groups bearing a proportionately high share of the unemployment burden. If 125,000 jobs were added for each 0.5-percent increment in the unemployment rate, such a program could employ approximately 25 percent of those unemployed in excess of the 4.5 percent trigger level. A program of this type would cost approximately $3 billion per year at 6 percent unemployment, assuming an expenditure of $8,000 per job.[7]

The Republicans in control of the Executive Branch in the Nixon (and then the Ford) administration were more cautious and less enthusiastic about their support for a larger Public Employment Program. Nevertheless, in the *Manpower Report of the President: 1975* the following answer is provided to the question—PEP: did it reach the mark?

With so many aims, it was inevitable that, if PEP accomplished some things, it would leave others undone. Several results stand out:

—PEP was too small to materially affect national unemployment totals or rates. While there was some evidence that the program could be stepped up in scale with positive effects, the results of PEP as a countercyclical program were not really significant.
—There was plenty of room on State and local employment rosters for PEP employees. Useful work was done with a minimum of inefficiency, and more intensive hiring did not appear to overtake the limits of expansion of public services.
—PEP exerted no major impact on public hiring policies and provided little training beyond job-acquired and related skills.
—The concept of decentralized responsibility for design and implementation was justified, as the national goals were generally realized in the aggregate, though local areas used the money in widely divergent ways.
—To a certain extent, the record of PEP counterbalanced the

negative stereotype public employment had carried since the New Deal. At least, it demonstrated that a modest, well-designed program could be popular and reasonably effective.[8]

Clearly, there had been a change in attitude from the "make-work" accusation of Nixon's 1970 veto message.

PART FOUR
PROGRAM CONTINUATION

15

CETA AND
EMERGENCY JOBS

The Emergency Employment Act of 1971 authorized a two-year program, and as this period entered its final six months the debate over public-service employment was renewed. In his Budget Message of January, 1973, President Nixon stated:

> Since the program began, unemployment has fallen and the financial ability of State and local governments to meet demand for services has improved. Most of the remaining unemployed need more assistance than is possible under this program and they can be more effectively served by regular manpower training programs.[1]

However, in that month 4.4 million Americans remained unemployed, and most congressional Democrats wanted to maintain a Public Employment Program. Senator Dominick had been right during the Senate debate of 1971 when he said that once an emergency program started its proponents would want to continue it. The program's supporters would not deny this claim, for that indeed was their intention.

On February 3, 1973, Representative Dominick Daniels introduced a bill, H. R. 4024, to extend the Emergency Employment Act for two more years, with minor amendments. His subcommittee held seven days of hearings[2] and reported the bill favorably to the full Education and Labor Committee, which in turn endorsed it.[3] After obtaining a rule, this bill came up for consideration in the

169

House of Representatives on April 18.[4] However, this was at a time when some southern Democrats were once again in revolt against the House leadership, and they joined with conservative Republicans to stymie action through a procedural maneuver. Toward the end of July the Education and Labor Committee reported a new version of the bill to extend the Emergency Employment Act (H. R. 7949), but it did not reach the floor before the August recess.[5]

By then, however, the Senate had acted. On April 12, 1973, Senators Nelson and Javits introduced a bill, S. 1560, to extend the Emergency Employment Act with only minor changes for another two years. A companion bill, S. 1559, dealt with reform of other manpower programs. Nelson's subcommittee held six days of hearings on these bills[6] and presented modifications of the two bills to the Senate Labor and Public Welfare Committee, which made some further changes and reported both bills to the Senate.[7] The Senate passed S. 1559 on July 24 by a vote of 88 to 5,[8] and S. 1560 on July 31 by a vote of 74 to 21.[9]

When Congress returned after the August recess, the House Education and Labor Committee did not ask for a rule in order to bring up H. R. 7949 to extend the Emergency Employment Act. Instead it turned its attention once again to manpower reform, with reasonable prospects that legislation could be adopted and signed by the President.

At this time, the unemployment rate was going down, dipping below 5 percent in June and reaching 4.5 percent in October, the lowest rate since March, 1970, in contrast to the 6 percent rate which had prevailed in 1971.

The big economic issues of 1973 were runaway inflation and a badly deteriorated international financial situation. The Nixon administration unfroze, refroze, and then thawed prices and wages, as its economic policies went through several phases. The President also impounded funds appropriated by Congress, and this became a major arena of dispute between Congress and the Executive Branch. This contest drew more attention from congressional leadership than specific programs.

To be sure, the same groups which had pushed for public-service employment in 1971 were in favor of continuation of the program: the AFL-CIO, the U. S. Conference of Mayors, the National League of Cities, the National Governors Conference, and the National Urban Coalition. A notable addition was the National Association of Counties, which had not been particularly involved in 1971 but which had become a devoted supporter of the program after counties handled 30 percent of PEP funds.

In the continuing debate, the technical arguments against public-service employment had been dissipated. Experience had shown that there were indeed plenty of tasks to be done without creating "make-work" and "dead-end jobs," and that the people so employed were productive and met public-service needs which would otherwise go unfulfilled. Issues such as wage levels, proportion of professional employment, and veterans preference had been resolved. Even the issue of transition seemed no longer to be a matter of great importance, particularly after the Labor Department played it down in program administration and adopted a job freeze which was a disincentive for transition.

What remained were the philosophical issues, particularly questions about the role of the federal government in the economy and the level of federal spending. Personal values are at the root of such issues, and rarely does concrete experience alter this base of opinion. Thus, President Nixon, George Shultz, in 1973 secretary of the treasury instead of director of the Office of Management and Budget, and Herbert Stein at the Council of Economic Advisers still opposed this kind of federal intervention except as an emergency measure. In mid-1973 they saw no such emergency, either political or economic. Congressional Democrats were of opposite persuasion, and so, on the philosophical issues, it was 1970 and 1971 all over again.

But 1973 was different because of the Watergate scandals. As revelation followed revelation, as top presidential aides resigned, and as a special committee under the chairmanship of Senator Sam Ervin of North Carolina conducted televised hearings, confrontation between Congress and President focused on issues arising from Watergate. This harrowing event also softened many of the hard stands taken by President Nixon and his appointees, setting the stage for compromises on legislation, including manpower reform.

Thus, in the spring of 1973 a new assistant secretary of labor for manpower, William Kolberg, took a firm stand against the Nelson-Javits manpower reform bill, still insisting upon the administration's revenue-sharing proposal. But in the fall he and his aides were working closely with Democratic and Republican leaders of the House Education and Labor Committee to work out a bill satisfactory to all parties. This was accomplished, and on November 21 Chairman Perkins reported a bill, H. R. 11010,[10] which increased the authority of state and local governmental prime sponsors over consolidated manpower programs. Public-service employment would be one of several eligible components, and in addition the bill provided special funds for public-service employment in local areas of high unemployment (patterned after Section 6 of the Emergency Employment Act). For this purpose $250 million would be authorized for 1974, and $500 million annually for the following three years. Over the objections of the administration and the House Republicans, the Democratic leadership insisted that funds be specifically reserved for the special-employment program, and the House of Representatives supported this position by a vote of 292 to 107 on November 28.[11]

The House amendments went to the Senate, which combined and substituted the language of its two bills, S. 1559 and S. 1560, except the Senators dropped their push for an extension of the Emergency Employment Act with $1 billion authorized and accepted the House's version.[12] The Senate lowered to 6 percent the unemployment level required to qualify a local area for the special public-employment program. The House had specified 7 percent, and the conference committee agreed upon 6.5 percent.[13] Both houses adopted the conference bill, which authorized not less than $250 million for public-service employment for the 1974 fiscal year, and not less than $350 million for 1975.[14] This figure was a true compromise for both the administration and congressional advocates of public-service employment.

The Comprehensive Employment and Training Act of 1973 (CETA), which President Nixon signed on December 28, was not remarkably different from the bill he had vetoed in December,

1970. It contained public-service employment funds and consolidated various manpower programs under local and state prime
sponsors, but it also made provision for several categorical programs (such as Indians, migrants, youth, older workers, offenders,
and persons of limited English-speaking ability). There were many
differences in details but not in basic principles.

Two political factors were influential. The first was Watergate.
The second was the prospect of higher unemployment, for the unemployment rate had risen in November and December—and this
before the energy crisis had begun to have its effect. Many econo-
mists were predicting a return to the 6 percent level of 1971, and
some thought it might go even higher. So President Nixon and his
advisers recognized that it would be useful to have a Public Employment Program available, and congressional supporters of more
public-service jobs concluded that a compromise bill would at least
continue the program—which they could expand later.

Indeed, simultaneously with implementation of the new act a
persistent push for program expansion occurred. Throughout 1974
and through the first half of 1975 (when the present narrative ends)
the continuing drama of public-service employment kept shifting
from one stage to another. There were three primary arenas of
action: administration, legislative authorization, and appropriations. The administrative arena involved internal operations of the
Labor Department and departmental relationships with local and
state CETA prime sponsors. The arena of legislative authorization
encompassed the two labor committees, their subcommittees, and
action on floor of the House of Representatives and the Senate. The
funding arena brought in the President and his budget advisers and
the appropriations committees of Congress, which came to play a
larger role in the expansion of the Public Employment Program.

Although CETA funds would not be available until July 1, 1974,
the Labor Department had to decide early in the year which local
jurisdictions were eligible to become prime sponsors and how much
money they would be allocated. Local and prime state sponsors had
to organize and draw up their plans for comprehensive manpower
programs (Title I) and for public-service employment (Title II).
By the middle of January the department had adopted a timetable

for implementation of CETA and had drafted some preliminary regulations. The various public interest groups—the National League of Cities/U. S. Conference of Mayors, the National Association of Counties, the National Governors Conference—had comments to offer, and so did congressional-committee staff. The most controversial issue was the old bugaboo "transition," which again reared its head. The draft regulations talked about an average length of subsidized employment of no longer than twelve months, but when congressional staff objected that Congress had placed no time limit on participation, the regulations were changed to provide a goal (not a requirement) of either placing half of the cumulative participants in unsubsidized employment or else placing participants in half the suitable vacancies of the public employer which are not filled by promotion. With the publication of the official regulations in the Federal Register on March 19, the CETA program was ready to roll.[15]

By then the cry for expansion of public-service employment was already being heard. For instance, toward the end of January, Kenneth Young, an AFL-CIO lobbyist, in an interview with the Mutual Broadcasting System, indicated that his organization intended to push for more funds for this program.[16] On February 8, Senator Javits introduced the first employment bill of the session, called the "Emergency Energy Employment Assistance Act of 1974," to tie into the current national crisis; it would authorize $4 billion for public-service jobs over a two-year period.[17] On the same day, at a hearing of the Joint Economic Committee, Javits asked Secretary of the Treasury Shultz for the administration's current view, and Shultz acknowledged: "We should have a variety of measures in mind which might be useful, and among those the President is quite ready to consider public service employment as one remedy."[18] A month later, when the Joint Economic Committee issued its recommendations on the President's Economic Report, it advocated a permanent public-service employment program, as previously cited.[19]

However, the crucial action for program expansion came not through the authorizing process but through appropriations. In his budget for the 1975 fiscal year, President Nixon requested $2.050

billion to fund the new Comprehensive Employment and Training Act, including $350 million for Title II, the Pubic Employment Program.[20] The President also asked for a supplemental appropriation of $250 million to fund Title II for the remainder of fiscal 1974. Both amounts were at the level of CETA-authorized action. Since Congress had previously extended funding for the Emergency Employment Act of 1971 into fiscal 1974, the President assumed that no more EEA funds would be required, now that CETA was law.

Congress, however, took a different stance. In April, the House Appropriations Committee reported a supplemental appropriations bill to provide the requested $250 million for CETA Title II (earmarked for areas with unemployment above 6.5 percent), and also threw in another $100 million to continue the old EEA Section 5 program (serving areas with 4.5 percent and more unemployment).[21] When this bill reached the House floor the members voted 236 to 168 to add another $150 million to the Section 5 fund, making a total of $500 million for public-service employment.[22] A few weeks later the Senate Appropriations Committee upped the ante by authorizing $825 million as supplemental appropriations for the public-service jobs,[23] and the whole Senate concurred.[24] The conference committee worked out a compromise of $620 million —$370 million for CETA Title II and $250 million for EEA Section 5; there was also a separate $306 million for summer youth jobs.[25] This bill passed both houses of Congress,[26] and President Nixon signed it on June 8, 1974.[27] The Labor Department allocated most of the new money to prime sponsors in July, but held back some of it in a discretionary fund.

By then the appropriations committees were well into their work on the 1975 budget. CETA funds would be part of the Labor-HEW appropriations bill. With money from the 1974 supplemental appropriations not yet flowing, the House Appropriations Committee saw no need to increase CETA Title II funding above the $350 million in the President's budget. However, the committee put in $100 million more in Title I and indicated that prime sponsors would use this for public-service employment.[28] The House stayed with the amount proposed for Title II but added $300 million more for other titles, bringing the 1975 CETA appropriations to $2.45

billion, $400 million above what the President had requested.[29]

Labor Department officials told the Senate Appropriations Committee that CETA prime sponsors were moving too slowly to be able to spend this extra $400 million, so the committee reduced it to a $100 million increase over the presidential budget—$50 million for Title II and $50 million for other titles.[30] In September, the Senate stayed with the committee's figure of $400 million for Title II but increased Title I by another $175 million, bringing the CETA total to $2.325 billion.[31]

Because the conference committee became bogged down in other issues in the Labor-HEW appropriations bill, and also because of the fall elections, Congress did not pass this legislation until December. At one point while the conference committee was meeting, Assistant Secretary of Labor Wiliam Kolberg warned of a presidential veto if Title II funding was increased.[32] The Senate conferees stood firm, however, and when the conference report with $400 million for Title II got to the floor of Congress, members had a letter of endorsement from Secretary of Labor Peter J. Brennan. The total for CETA was compromised at $2.4 billion, $350 million more than the budget request. Conferees indicated that at least $280 million in Title I was intended for public-service employment.[33] With this settled, both houses voted their approval on November 26.[34] President Gerald R. Ford signed the Labor-HEW appropriations act containing CETA funds on December 7.[35]

Ford had assumed the presidency in August, following the resignation of Richard M. Nixon. Like his predecessor, Ford saw inflation, not unemployment, as the primary economic problem of the United States. In response, he scheduled a series of economic conferences in September to consult with a broad range of American leadership. Although inflation received major attention at the first meeting, on September 11, the new President announced the release of the remainder of public-service employment funds from the supplemental appropriations. About a month later, he appeared before a joint session of Congress to make recommendations about economic policy. Inflation continued to be his principal concern, but he did recommend a new Community Improvement Program of short-term public jobs for persons who had exhausted unemploy-

ment insurance and an extended unemployment-insurance program.[36] Legislation to this effect was introduced by Representatives
Esch and Quie[37] and Senator Taft.[38]

During the President's economic conferences, a number of persons argued that unemployment should take equal billing with inflation as a worrisome economic problem. Black leaders underscored this concern by holding their own summit conference, which
demanded a massive public-employment program. The anxiety of
many people over jobs grew when the Bureau of Labor Statistics
reported early in October that the unemployment rate in September
was 5.8 percent, slightly more than one percentage point above the
previous year, and steadily rising. On Capitol Hill the Joint Economic Committee added its voice and issued a report calling for
400,000 to 650,000 public-service jobs.[39]

Once again the authorizing committees sprang into action—the
House Select Labor Subcommittee chaired by Representative
Daniels and the Senate Subcommittee on Employment, Poverty, and
Migratory Labor chaired by Senator Nelson. They had before them
several proposals: the President's program; House bills introduced
by Representative Daniels, Marvin L. Esch of Michigan (ranking
Republican on the subcommittee), William S. Moorhead of Pennsylvania, and Lionel Vander Veen of Michigan;[40] and Senate bills
introduced by Senator Javits (pending since February) and Nelson.[41] In November, Representative Augustus F. Hawkins of California came in with a new version of his Equal Opportunity and Full
Employment Act,[42] a vastly larger program than the others, and
Senator Hubert H. Humphrey of Minnesota introduced a similar
measure in the Senate.[43]

During the first half of October, the Daniels subcommittee held
five days of public hearings and then marked up the chairman's bill,
H. R. 16596.[44] The full Committee on Education and Labor considered the proposal and reported it out with authorization for $2
billion in public-service jobs.[45] The House of Representatives
adopted the measure by a vote of 322 to 53 on December 12, and
also incorporated provisions to extend unemployment-insurance
benefits to unemployed persons not previously covered.[46]

On the Senate side, the Nelson subcommittee held hearings for three days and also used its chairman's bill, S. 4079, for mark-up.[47] The subcommittee agreed to $4 billion for public-service employment and added a title extending unemployment-insurance benefits.[48] The bill then moved through the full Committee on Labor and Public Welfare in time to reach the Senate floor on the same day the House was considering its bill. Senator James A. McClure, a Republican from Idaho, persuaded the Senate to add $1 billion in authorization for a job-opportunities program of public-works projects, to be administered by the Commerce Department. With this amendment, S. 4079 passed, 79 to 13.[49]

With the unemployment rate increased to 6.6 percent and adjournment near, the conference committee worked swiftly. In less than a week it produced a compromise figure of $2.5 billion for an emergency-jobs program. With a name variation, it resembled Section 5 of the Emergency Employment Act of 1971 and became Title VI of the Comprehensive Employment and Training Act. The conference committee also incorporated the unemployment-insurance provisions, and the Senate's Job Opportunities Program, scaled down to $500 million authorized.[50] The House of Representatives and the Senate both voted favorably on the conference bill on December 18,[51] and President Ford affixed his signature on the last day of 1974.[52]

Simultaneously, the appropriations committees produced a supplemental appropriations act of $4 billion, including $875 million for the Emergency Jobs Program and $125 million for the Job Opportunities Program.[53] President Ford signed the act on January 3, 1975.[54]

With a renewed sense of urgency, the Labor Department was already shifting gears to implement the Emergency Jobs Program. This was a shift because throughout the year the department and most of the prime sponsors had not been moving very fast to carry out the Public Employment Program of CETA Title II. In November, Assistant Secretary Kolberg accused the prime sponsors of foot-dragging. Organizations of local and state officials cited the difficulties of working within tight budgets caused by the spreading recession and of having to lay off public employees at the same time others were being hired under the Public Employment Program.

They also countercharged that the Labor Department's unrealistic transition requirements and cumbersome administrative regulations were holding back hiring. On balance, it appears that bureaucratic processes on both sides retarded the program and prevented the kind of rapid hiring which had occurred in the fall of 1971, under the Emergency Employment Act, when procedures were simple and enthusiasm fresh for a new program.

Nevertheless, by December, 1974, the pace had begun to pick up. Even before the Emergency Jobs Program was finally enacted, the Labor Department had its regional office staff in for a briefing and instructed them to be in touch with prime sponsors by the end of the month. Draft regulations came out the last week in December and were finalized on January 10.[55] They indicated that the Title VI program would have placement goals but no strict transition requirement—a matter made abundantly clear by Congress in the legislation. An interim allocation was made early in January and final allocations followed a few weeks later. Although federal officials and representatives of local and state government continued their exchanges about who was delaying the program, hiring proceeded rapidly. By the end of April 324,000 persons held jobs in public-service employment, including 12,500 financed by CETA Title I, 167,000 by Title II, 117,700 by Title VI, and 26,800 by CETA transitional provisions for the Emergency Employment Act of 1971. This was twice the peak level of EEA jobs three years earlier.

Program acceleration revealed that some of the same issues raised by the Emergency Employment Act were still alive, particularly those involving labor unions and civil service. The problem was aggravated by widespead layoffs of public employees. In order to assure maintenance of local effort and to prevent the Emergency Jobs Program from becoming merely a revenue-sharing measure, the act and the regulations prohibited laying-off employees for purpose of transferring them to the new program. However, bonafide layoffs could be rehired. Unions of public employees pressed for emergency jobs for its laid-off members, urged that other persons hired under the program be assigned mainly entry-level jobs and zealously guarded against violation of promotional rights of their members. These issues, however, did not prevent filling virtually all the jobs made available by the program.[56]

There was no shortage of applicants, and in a few places there were near riots as hundreds crowded in to apply for the relatively few jobs available. No wonder, for the national unemployment rate hit 7.9 percent in January, 1975, and reached 8.9 percent in May, and in many cities it was much higher. So naturally members of Congress pressed for an even larger program. Representatives Daniels, Hawkins, and Esch and Senators Javits and Nelson all introduced bills calling for $5 billion and more for public-service employment.[57] The two subcommittees chaired by Daniels and Nelson began another round of hearings on these measures.

Once again the appropriations committees picked up the action as it worked on another supplemental appropriations bill. Although President Ford had included no additional money for the Emergency Jobs Program in the federal budget he submitted to Congress in January, 1975, two months later he indicated a willingness to add $1.625 billion for emergency jobs and $412.7 million for summer youth employment. These were the amounts the House Appropriations Committee had already placed in its bill, and the committee also added over $3 billion more in job-creating public-works projects.[58] A proposal for $250 million in jobs for railroad maintenance was knocked out on the House floor on a point of order. With only a couple of minor amendments, a majority of the House adopted the rest of the supplemental appropriations bill on March 12.[59]

Quickly the Senate Appropriations Committee moved into action, held hearings, and reported a bill, which the full Senate took up on April 25.[60] The Senate accepted the $1.625 billion for emergency jobs, added $89.6 million to the summer youth-employment program, restored the rail-improvement program, and made some other changes which brought the total to new budget authority of $5.5 billion.[61] This was $131 million above the House bill and $3.5 billion over the administration requests, mainly because of the additional public-works projects.

As the conference committee met, veto threats came from the White House and the Labor Department, but this did not deter the conferees from producing a bill which appropriated $5.3 billion in new funds. They split the difference on youth employment, stuck with $1.625 billion for emergency jobs, and kept the various public-works projects, but they provided no money for rail improvements.[62] The Emergency Employment Appropriations Act of 1975 passed the House on May 14 and the Senate on May 16.[63]

However, President Ford strenuously objected to the public-works provisions and to the additional $3 billion beyond his request. So he vetoed the act on May 28. The House on June 4 voted, 277 to 145, to override, but this was three votes short of the two-thirds majority required by the Constitution and the veto was sustained.[64]

Within a week Congress passed a separate appropriations bill of $456 million for summer youth jobs (the amount from the vetoed bill),[65] and the President signed it.[66] Then Congress added the $1.625 billion for emergency employment to a joint resolution making continuing appropriation for the fiscal year 1976,[67] and this too was accepted by the President.[68] There would be enough money to keep approximately 310,000 people working in public-service employment through the end of 1976.

These appropriation acts passed by Congress and signed by President Ford symbolized the solid acceptance of public-service employment as one tool in the array of policy instruments available for dealing with economic fluctuations. By this standard, the Emergency Employment Act of 1971 and the descendant programs could be deemed a success. Like social security, medicare, and other once-controversial programs, public-service employment had, through proven experience, passed the test of time and gained acceptance.

But matters of controversy remained. Precisely what role public-service employment should play in the total picture was still in dispute. The appropriations battle in the spring of 1975 revealed that Congress wanted additional kinds of job-creation measures in the form of public works. President Ford's veto indicated that, in working out a tax cut with Congress earlier in the year, he had gone as far as he would in building up the federal deficit. He would support a limited public-service employment program and extended unemployment insurance, but not public works. Meanwhile, city and county officials pressed for an emergency general revenue-sharing fund to help local government through the recession—not as a substitute for public-service employment but as yet another approach to dealing with economic problems.

The proper level of public-service employment also remained in dispute. Although the consensus figure of $1.625 billion emerged in the appropriations battle in the spring of 1975, members of Congress at the same time were pressing for a much larger authorization. In January, 1975, Representative Hawkins introduced a new version of his Equal Opportunity and Full Employment Act.[69] In February, Representative Daniels presented a bill authorizing $5 billion for the 1976 fiscal year for Title VI of CETA,[70] and his subcommittee held hearings on the proposal. In March, Representative Esch, the ranking Republican on the subcommittee, introduced a bill extending Title VI another year.[71] In July, the Daniels subcommittee completed mark-up of a bill thoroughly revising the Title VI program and authorizing more public-service jobs. This bill was waiting action by the full Labor and Education Committee in September, 1975, as this narrative ends.

On the Senate side, in February, 1975, Senator Javits introduced two bills, one containing his ideas for full employment, and another which would authorize up to $7.8 billion for CETA Title VI during the 1976 fiscal year.[72] In May, Senator Nelson, with the cosponsorship of Senators Javits, Williams, Cranston, Mondale, Humphrey, Kennedy, Randolph, and Pell, introduced a measure to authorize as much as $5 billion in 1976 for emergency jobs.[73] Nelson's subcommittee then opened hearings on this and other pending bills as the first step in a legislative strategy aimed at expansion of public-service employment. The subcommittee expected to get to mark-up in September and October, 1975.

Lurking in the background was the issue of whom public-service employment should benefit. Many of the early advocates, going back to the proposed but defeated Emergency Employment Act of 1967, saw the program as serving mostly disadvantaged persons, such as poorly educated minorities, unemployed youth, and others who have difficulty getting jobs even in good times. Language of this sort was included in the Emergency Employment Act of 1971 and in the Comprehensive Employment and Training Act of 1973, and Title II of the latter was aimed particularly at areas with substantial unemployment and at the disadvantaged persons. However, the much larger program of Title VI, aided by the Emergency Jobs and Unemployment Assistance Act of 1974, was intended to serve normally employed persons who were out of work because of the recession. In the spring of 1975 the Labor Department had virtually merged Titles II and VI administratively with the result that emphasis on disadvantaged persons was played down. This concerned some members of Congress and committee staff who were watchdogging the program, indicating that this issue was likely to remain a matter of controversy in the foreseeable future.

No, the debate over job creation through public-service employment had not ended. Nevertheless, the Emergency Employment Act of 1971 had clearly opened the door to a continuing program of public jobs, federally financed but administered by local and state governments. The Comprehensive Employment and Training Act of 1973 kept the program going on a reduced scale, and then the Emergency Jobs and Unemployment Assistance Act of 1974 expanded the program to cope with a deeper recession. In this manner, four years of public-service employment involving all levels of government had written a new chapter in the continuing saga of American federalism.

NOTES

Prologue

1. *Public Papers of the Presidents: Richard Nixon, 1970* (Washington: U. S. Government Printing Office, 1972), p. 1,141.

2. *Public Papers of the Presidents: Richard Nixon, 1971* (Washington: U. S. Government Printing Office, 1973), p. 816.

3. *Economic Report of the President, 1970* and *Annual Report of the Council of Economic Advisers* (Washington: U. S. Government Printing Office, 1970), pp. 90, 92.

4. Ibid., p. 5.

5. *Economic Report of the President, 1953* (Washington: U. S. Government Printing Office, 1953), p. 19.

Chapter 1. Public-Employment Proposals in the Sixties

1. U. S. Senate, Commission on Labor and Public Welfare, Subcommittee on Employment and Manpower, *Toward Full Employment: Proposals for a Comprehensive Employment and Manpower Policy for the United States.* 88th Congress, 2nd Session (Washington: U. S. Government Printing Office, 1964).

2. U. S. Senate, Committee on Labor and Public Welfare, *Economic Opportunity Amendments of 1967*, Senate Report No. 563, 90th Congress, 1st Session, 1967.

3. *Congressional Record,* daily ed., Oct. 4, 1967, S. 14123.

4. The survey results were published by Harold L. Sheppard in *The Nature of the Job Problem and the Role of New Public Service Employment* (Kalamazoo, Mich.: W. E. Upjohn Institute for Employment Research, 1969).

Chapter 2. Legislative Action in 1969 and 1970

1. *Public Papers of the President: Richard Nixon, 1969* (Washington: U. S. Government Printing Office, 1971), pp. 22-23.

2. Ibid., p. 254.

3. H. R. 10908, 91st Congress, First Session.

4. H. R. 11620, 91st Congress, First Session.

5. *Public Papers of the President: Richard Nixon, 1969* (Washington: U. S. Government Printing Office, 1971), pp. 659–662.

6. S. 2838, H. R. 13472, 91st Congress, First Session.

7. U. S. Senate, Committee on Labor and Public Welfare, Subcommittee on Employment, Manpower and Poverty, *Manpower Development and Training Legislation, 1970*, 91st Congress, First and Second sessions, 1970, 4 vols.

8. S. 3878, 91st Congress, Second Session.

9. U. S. Senate Committee on Labor and Public Welfare, *Employment and Training Opportunities Act of 1970*, S. Rept. 91–1136, 91st Congress, Second Session, 1970.

10. *Congressional Record,* daily ed., Sept. 16–17, 1970, pp. S15720–70, S15856–912.

11. U. S. House of Representatives, Committee on Education and Labor, Select Subcommittee on Labor, *Manpower Act of 1969*, 91st Congress, Second Session, 1970, 2 vols.

12. U. S. House of Representatives, Committee on Education and Labor, *Comprehensive Manpower Act of 1970*, House Report 91-1557, 91st Congress, Second Session, 1970.

13. *Congressional Record*, daily ed., Nov. 17, 1970, pp. H 10362–443.

14. U. S. House of Representatives, *The Employment and Manpower Act*, House Report 91-1713, 91st Congress, Second Session, 1970.

15. *Congressional Record*, daily ed., Dec. 9-10, 1970, pp. S19852–77 and S19952–59.

16. Ibid. H 11508-16.

17. *Public Papers of the President: Richard Nixon, 1970* (Washington: U. S. Government Printing Office, 1972), p. 1,142.

18. *Congressional Record*, daily ed., Dec. 21, 1970, pp. S 20966–91.

Chapter 3. Passage of the Emergency Employment Act of 1971

1. U. S. Senate, Committee on Labor and Public Welfare, Subcommittee on Employment, Manpower, and Poverty, *Emergency Employment Act of 1971*, 92nd Congress, First Session, 1971.

2. *Public Papers of the President: Richard Nixon, 1971* (Washington: U. S. Government Printing Office, 1973), p. 50–58.

3. Senate Hearings (see footnote 1, above), pp. 208–239.

4. S. 1234, 92nd Congress, First Session.

5. U. S. Senate, Committee on Labor and Public Welfare, *Emergency Employment Act of 1971*, Senate Report 92-48, 92nd Congress, First Session, 1971.

6. Congressional Record, daily ed., Apr. 1, 1971, pp. S 4306–48.

7. U. S. House of Representatives, Committee on Education and Labor, Select Subcommittee on Labor, *Emergency Employment Act of 1971*, 92nd Congress, First Session, 1971.

8. Ibid., p. 246.

9. Ibid., p. 252.

10. Ibid., p. 253.

11. U. S. House of Representatives, Committee on Education and Labor, *Emergency Employment Act of 1971*, House Report 92-176, 92nd Congress, Second Session, 1971.

12. *Congressional Record,* daily edition, May 18, 1971, pp. H 4047 –9.

13. Ibid., May 18, 1971, pp. H 4036–59; June 1, 1971, pp. H 4461 –73; June 2, 1971, pp. H 4504–39.

14. *Public Papers of the President: Richard Nixon, 1970* (Washington: U. S. Government Printing Office, 1972), p. 454.

15. Arthur F. Burns, *The Basis for Lasting Prosperity,* Address at Pepperdine College, Los Angeles, Calif., Dec. 7, 1970.

16. U. S. House of Representatives, *Emergency Employment Act,* House Report 92-310, 92nd Congress, First Session, 1971.

17. *Congressional Record,* daily ed., p. S 10271.

18. Ibid., July 1, 1971, pp. S 10162–77.

19. Ibid., July 1, 1971, pp. H 6224–9.

20. *Public Papers of the President: Richard Nixon, 1971* (Washington: U. S. Government Printing Office, 1973), p. 816.

Chapter 4. Choosing the Beneficiaries

1. U. S. Senate, Committee on Labor and Public Welfare, *Emergency Employment Act of 1971,* Senate Report. 92-48, 92nd Congress, First Session, 1971.

2. *Congressional Record,* daily ed., Apr. 1, 1971, p. S 4321.

3. U. S. House of Representatives, Committee on Education and Welfare, *Emergency Employment Act of 1971,* House Report 92-176, 92nd Congress, First Session, 1971.

4. U. S. House of Representatives, *Emergency Employment Act,* House Report 92-310, 92nd Congress, First Session, 1971.

5. S. 31, H. R. 3613, 92nd Congress, First Session, 1971.

6. U. S. Senate, Committee on Labor and Public Welfare, *Emergency Employment Act of 1971,* Senate Report 92-48, 92nd Congress, First Session, 1971.

7. Emergency Employment Act of 1971, Public Law 92-54.

8. Comptroller General of the United States, *Review of the Allocation of Funds for the Public Employment Program Under the Emergency Employment Act of 1971* (U. S. General Accounting Office, Dec. 17, 1971).

9. U. S. House of Representatives, Committee on Appropriations, *Emergency Employment Assistance Appropriations, for Fiscal Year 1972,* 92nd Congress, First Session, 1971.

10. *Congressional Record,* daily ed., Aug. 4, 1971, pp. H 7852–71.

11. U. S. Senate, Committee on Appropriations, *Emergency Employment Assistance Appropriations, Fiscal Year 1972,* 92nd Congress, First Session, 1971.

12. *Congressional Record,* daily ed., Aug. 6, 1971, pp. S 13592–97.

Chapter 5. Federal Administration

1. Stanley H. Ruttenberg, *Manpower Challenge of the 1970s: Institutions and Social Change* (Baltimore: The Johns Hopkins University Press, 1970), pp. 74–97.

2. U. S. Department of Labor, Office of Information, *Hodgson Sets Guidelines for Public Service Employment Program,* news release dated July 23, 1971.

3. U. S. Department of Labor, Office of Information, *Labor Department announces Funds to Localities and States for Public Jobs* (Aug. 12, 1971).

4. *Federal Register,* vol. 36, no. 158 (Aug. 14, 1971), pp. 15,433–37.

5. U. S. Department of Labor, Manpower Administration, *Emergency Employment Act: Program Guidelines* (Aug. 27, 1971).

6. U. S. Department of Labor, Manpower Administration, *Program Guidelines for Section 6 of the Emergency Employment Act* (Sept. 20, 1971).

7. U. S. Department of Labor, Manpower Administration, *Program Guidelines for Reservation Indians, Emergency Employment Act* (Sept. 27, 1971).

8. U. S. Department of Labor, Manpower Administration, *Program Guidelines for the High Impact Demonstration Program of the Emergency Employment Act* (Oct. 13, 1971).

Chapter 6. City Programs

1. Most of the case studies used in these three chapters were produced for the National Manpower Policy Task Force and are contained in the following publications: *The Emergency Employment Act: An Interim Assessment* (1972), *The Emergency Employment Act: Second Interim Assessment* (1972), and *Case Studies of the Emergency Employment Act in Operation* (1973). The first and third were printed by the U. S. Senate, Committee on Labor and Public Welfare, Subcommittee on Employment, Manpower and Poverty; the second was published by the National Manpower Policy Task Force.

2. National League of Cities/U. S. Conference of Mayors, *Public Employment Program and the Cities*, vol. 2: *Special Report* (1973), p. 12.

3. This and subsequent reference to New York is derived from a case study by Marilyn Gittell contained in *An Interim Assessment*, pp. 245–56; *Second Interim Assessment*, pp. 30–35; *Case Studies*, pp. 885–964.

4. Chicago case study by Myron Roomkin in *An Interim Assessment*, pp. 105–28; *Second Assessment*, pp. 71–80; *Case Studies*, pp. 329–412.

5. Milwaukee case study by Peter Kobrak in *An Interim Assessment*, pp. 208–34; *Second Assessment*, pp. 45–53; *Case Studies*, pp. 641–756.

6. San Diego case study by Marjorie S. Turner in *Second Assessment*, pp. 108–16; *Case Studies*, pp. 121–244.

7. Winston-Salem case study by George B. Autry and Bob Smith in *Progress Report on the Emergency Employment Act in North Carolina* (North Carolina Manpower Development Corporation, January, 1972) and in *Second Interim Assessment*, pp. 81–86; *Case Studies*, pp. 965–1,054.

8. Decatur case study by Roger Bezdak in *An Interim Assessment*, pp. 75–104 and by James Hribal in *Case Studies*, pp. 447–92.

9. National League of Cities/U. S. Conference of Mayors, *Public Employment Program and the Cities*, vol. 1: *Overview*; vol. 2: *Special Report*; vol. 3: *Case Studies* (1973).

Chapter 7. County, Substate-District, and Indian Programs

1. San Diego County case study by Marjorie S. Turner in *Second Assessment*, pp. 108–16; *Case Studies*, pp. 121–244.

2. Champaign County case study by Roger Bezdak and Alva R. Butler in *An Interim Assessment*, pp. 75–104; *Second Interim Assessment*, pp. 1–7; *Case Studies*, pp. 413–46.

3. Robeson County case study by George B. Autry and Bob Smith in *Progress Report on the Emergency Employment Act in North Carolina* (North Carolina Manpower Development Corporation, January, 1972) and in *Second Interim Assessment*, pp. 81–86; *Case Studies*, pp. 965–1,054.

4. Unpublished Bell County case study by Howard W. Hallman, Center for Governmental Studies, Washington, D.C.

5. South Texas Development Council case study by Vernon Briggs in *An Interim Assessment*, pp. 153–86; *Second Interim Assessment*, pp. 13–17; *Case Studies*, pp. 1,055–1,172.

6. Berkshire Manpower Commission case study by Michael Gwin and Leonard J. Hausman in *Case Studies*, pp. 533–640.

7. Montana Intertribal Policy Board case study by Robert F. Gwilliam in *Case Studies*, pp. 1,273–1,410.

8. Navajo Nation case study by Robert F. Gwilliam in *Case Studies*, pp. 1,273–1,410.

9. *Manpower at the National Association of Counties, 1972* (Washington: National Association of Counties, 1972).

Chapter 8. State Programs

1. North Carolina case study by George B. Autry and Bob Smith in *Progress Report on the Emergency Employment Act in North Carolina* (North Carolina Manpower Development Corporation, January, 1972) and in *Second Interim Assessment*, pp. 81–86; *Case Studies*, pp. 965–1,054.

2. Utah case study by Garth L. Mangum and James Sawyer in *An Interim Assessment* pp. 257–74; *Second Interim Assessment*, pp. 54–63; *Case Studies*, 1,173–1,212.

3. Texas case study by Vernon Briggs in *An Interim Assessment*, pp. 153–84; *Second Interim Assessment*, pp. 8–13; *Case Studies*, pp. 1,055–1,172.

4. Illinois case study by Roger Bezdak in *An Interim Assessment*, pp. 75–104.

5. Missouri case study by David W. Stevens in *An Interim Assessment*, pp. 235–44; *Second Interim Assessment*, pp. 87–91; *Case Studies*, pp. 752–884.

6. California case study by Martin P. Oettinger and C. Daniel Venall in *Case Studies*, pp. 1–86.

Chapter 9. Demonstration Projects

1. U. S. Department of Labor, Office of Information, *Hodgson Allocates $115 Million for 25,000 Additional Public Jobs* (Oct. 8, 1971).

2. Case study by Roger Bezdak in *An Interim Assessment*, pp. 75 –104; *Second Interim Assessment*, pp. 1–7; and by James Hribal in *Case Studies*, pp. 447–92.

3. Case study by Roger Bezdak in *An Interim Assessment*, pp.75 –104; *Second Interim Assessment*, pp. 1–7; and by Ava Butler in *Case Studies*, pp. 413–46.

4. National Planning Association, *An Evaluation of the Economic Impact Demonstration Project of the Public Employment Program. Program Implementation*, Working Paper 1, 1972.

5. Auerbach Associates, *The Welfare Demonstration Program as a Social Experiment: An Interim Assessment* (1973).

Chapter 10. Civil Service and Public Employees' Unions

1. U. S. Civil Service Commission, Bureau of Intergovernmental Personnel Programs, *Interim Guidelines for Reevaluation of Employment Requirements and Practices Pursuant to Emergency Employment Act* (1971).

2. National Civil Service League, *Emergency Action Plan for Public Service Employment* (1971).

3. National League of Cities/U. S. Conference of Mayors, *Public Employment Program for the Cities*, vol. 3: *Case Studies* (1973).

4. Section 12(c), Emergency Employment Act of 1971, Public Law 92-54.

5. J. Joseph Loewenberg, Richard Leone, Karen S. Koziara, and Edward C. Koziara, *The Impact of Public Employee Unions on the Public Employment Program* (Temple University: Center for Labor and Manpower Studies, 1973), p. i.

6. Ibid., pp. D-1 to D-17.

7. Ibid., pp. F-1 to F-17.

8. Ibid., pp. H-1 to H-11.

9. Ibid., pp. 28–29.

Chapter 11. Information System, Monitoring, and Evaluation

1. U. S. Department of Labor, Manpower Administration, Office of Financial and Management Information Systems, *Agent Information System: Public Employment Program* (1972).

2. Westat, Inc., *Longitudinal Evaluation of the Public Employment Program and Validation of the PEP Data Bank,* Final Report, Apr., 1975.

3. National Planning Association, *An Evaluation of the Economic Impact Project of the Public Employment Program,* Final Report, 4 vols. May, 1974.

4. Decision Making Information (DMI), *Evaluation of the Emergency Employment Act Welfare Demonstration Project,* Final Report, April, 1975.

5. J. A. Reyes Associates, Inc., *The Public Employment Program: An Impact Assessment,* Final Report, August, 1974.

6. American Indian Consultants, *An Evaluation of the Public Employment Program for Reservation Indians* (1973).

7. Loewenberg, et al., op. cit. (see above, chap. 10, n. 5)

8. Martin Held and Richard P. Schick, *Transitional Employment: A Manpower Tool for State and Local Governments* (National Civil Service League, 1973).

9. Everett Crawford, *Transitional Employment: A Manpower Tool for State and Local Governments* (Washington: Center for Governmental Studies, 1973).

10. Comptroller General of the United States, Reports to the Subcommittee on Employment, Manpower, and Poverty, Committee on Labor and Public Welfare, United States Senate: *Review of the Allocation of Funds for the Public Employment Program Under the Emergency Employment Act of 1971* (Dec. 17, 1971); *Comparison of the Number of Persons Actually Hired by the Program Agents with Anticipated Hirings* (Feb. 16, 1972); *Report on the Preparation and Approval of Plans to Implement the Public Employment Program* (Mar. 17, 1973); *Selection and Enrollment of Participants* (Oct. 12, 1972); *Types of Jobs Offered to Unemployed Persons* (Nov. 27, 1972); *Impact of Grants to Indian Tribes* (Mar. 14, 1973); and *Public Service Benefits from Jobs* (June 8, 1973).

11. U. S. House of Representatives, Committee on Appropriations, *Departments of Labor and Health, Education and Welfare Appropriations for 1973,* 92nd Congress, 2nd Session, 1972, Part 6, pp. 17–20, 40–41, 51–53, 195–227.

12. Ibid., p. 213.

13. Ibid., p. 20.

14. U. S. Senate, Committee on Appropriation, *Departments of Labor and Health, Education, and Welfare and Related Agencies Appro-*

priations, Fiscal Year 1973, 92nd Congress, 2nd Session, 1972, Part 2, pp. 1,535–65.

15. Ibid., p. 1,545.

16. U. S. Senate, Committee on Labor and Public Welfare, Subcommittee on Employment, Manpower, and Poverty, *The Emergency Employment Act: An Interim Assessment,* 92nd Congress, 2nd Session, 1972.

17. National Manpower Policy Task Force, *The Emergency Employment Act, Second Interim Assessment, Case Studies of State and Local Experience* (Washington, D. C. 1972).

18. U. S. Senate, Committee on Labor and Public Welfare, Subcommittee on Employment, Poverty, and Migratory Labor, *Evaluation of the First 18 Months of the Public Employment Program,* 93rd Congress, First Session, 1973.

19. U. S. Senate Committee on Labor and Public Welfare, Subcommitee on Employment, Poverty and Migratory Labor, *Case Studies of the Emergency Employment Act in Operation,* 93rd Congress, First Session, 1973.

20. Sar A. Levitan and Robert Taggart, *Emergency Employment Act: The PEP Generation* (Salt Lake City: Olympus Publishing Co., 1974).

21. Nation Urban Coalition, *The Public Employment Program: An Evaluation* (1972).

Chapter 12. Participants and Their Jobs

1. Except where otherwise stated, all data in this chapter come from the U. S. Department of Labor, Manpower Administration, Agent Information System.

2. Westat, Inc., *Longitudinal Evaluation of the Public Employment Program and Validation of the PEP Data Bank,* Final Report, April, 1975, p. 47.

3. Ibid., p. 5–6.

4. National Urban Coalition, *The Public Employment Program: An Evaluation* (1972), p. 40.

5. Comptroller General of the United States, *Selection and Enrollment of Participants in Programs under the Emergency Employment Act of 1971* (U. S. General Accounting Office, 1972).

6. Sar A. Levitan and Robert Taggart, *Evaluation of the First 18 Months of the Public Employment Program* (Committee Print of the U. S. Senate Committee on Labor and Public Welfare, Subcommittee

on Employment, Poverty and Migratory Labor, 93rd Congress, First Session), (Washington: Government Printing Office, 1973), pp. 9–10.

7. National Urban Coalition, *The Public Employment Program: An Evaluation,* p. 7.

8. Levitan and Taggart, *Evaluation of the First 18 Months of the Public Employment Program,* p. 12.

9. Ibid.

10. *Manpower Report of the President: 1975,* p. 47.

11. Comptroller General of the United States, *Public Service Benefits from Jobs Under the Emergency Employment Act of 1971* (U. S. General Accounting Office, 1973).

12. *Manpower Report of the President: 1975.* p. 46.

13. National Urban Coalition, *The Public Employment Program: An Evaluation,* p. 28.

14. National Planning Association, *An Evaluation of the Economic Impact of the Public Employment Program,* Final Report (May 1974), vol. 1, pp. 4–6.

15. Ibid., p. 145.

16. Ibid., p. 124.

17. Ibid., p. 104.

18. Ibid., p. 22.

19. Ibid., p. 22.

20. Decision Making Information, *Evaluation: Emergency Employment Act Welfare Demonstration Project,* Final Report (April, 1975), pp. 15–16.

21. Ibid., p. 6.

22. Ibid., p. 16.

Chapter 13. Transitional Employment

1. U. S. Department of Labor, Manpower Administration, *Emergency Employment Act: Program Guidelines* (Aug. 27, 1971), Section IX. D.

2. Unless otherwise indicated, participant data in this chapter come from U. S. Department of Labor, Manpower Administration, Agent Information System.

3. Westat, Inc., *Longitudinal Evaluation of the Public Employment and Validation of the PEP Data Bank,* Final Report (April, 1975), pp. 5-19 to 5-25.

4. Ibid., p. 6-24.

5. Ibid., p. 6-15.

6. Ibid., p. 6-3.

7. Ibid., p. 6-59.

8. Ibid., p. 6-68.

9. Ibid., pp. 8-4 to 8-5.

10. Unpublished case study by Center for Governmental Studies, Washington, D.C.

11. National League of Cities/U. S. Conference of Mayors, *Public Employment Program and the Cities*, vol. 2: *Special Report* (1973), pp. 75–116.

12. Levitan and Tagart, *Evaluation of the First 18 Months of the Public Employment Program*, p. 40.

13. Everett Crawford, *Transitional Employment: A Manpower Tool for State and Local Governments*. (Washington: Center for Governmental Studies, 1973). Also see report with same title by Martin Held and Richard P. Schick (Washington: National Civil Service League, 1973).

14. National League of Cities/U. S. Conference of Mayors, *Public Employment Program and the Cities*, vol. 2: *Special Report*, p. 95.

Chapter 14. New Federalism and Institutional Change

1. *Public Papers of the Presidents: Lyndon Johnson, 1966* (Washington: U. S. Government Printing Office, 1967), pp. 1,366–67.

2. *Public Papers of the Presidents: Richard Nixon, 1969* (Washington: U. S. Government Printing Office, 1970), p. 324.

3. *Public Papers of the Presidents: Richard Nixon, 1970* (Washington: U. S. Government Printing Office, 1972), p. 1,141.

4. Sar A. Levitan and Robert Taggart, *Evaluation of the First 18 Months of the Public Employment Program*, p. 39.

5. Ibid., p. 40.

6. J. A. Reyes Associates, *The Public Employment Program: An Impact Assessment*, Final Report (August 1974), p. 5.

7. U. S. Congress, Joint Economic Committee, *The 1974 Joint Economic Report*, House Report No. 93-927, 93rd Congress, 2nd Session, 1974.

8. *Manpower Report of the President: 1975*, p. 49.

Chapter 15. CETA and Emergency Jobs

1. *The Budget of the United States Government, Fiscal Year 1974* (Washington: U. S. Government Printing Office, 1973), p. 131.

2. U. S. House of Representatives, Committee on Education and Labor, Select Subcommittee on Labor, *Emergency Employment Act Amendments of 1973,* 93rd Congress, 1st Session, 1973.

3. U. S. House of Representatives, Committee on Education and Labor, *Emergency Employment Amendments of 1973,* Report No. 93-142, 93rd Congress, 1st Session, 1973.

4. *Congressional Record,* daily ed., Apr. 18, 1973, H 2950-51.

5. U. S. House of Representatives, Committee on Education and Labor, *Emergency Employment Amendments of 1973,* Report No. 93-404, 93rd Congress, 1st Session, 1973.

6. U. S. Senate, Committee on Labor and Public Welfare, Subcommittee on Employment, Poverty, and Migratory Labor. *Job Training and Employment Legislation, 1973,* 93rd Congress, 1st Session, 1973.

7. U. S. Senate, Committee on Labor and Public Welfare, *Job Training and Community Services Act of 1973,* Report No. 93-304, and *Emergency Employment Amendments of 1973,* Report No. 93-305, 93rd Congress, 1st Session, 1973.

8. *Congressional Record,* daily ed., July 24, 1973, S 14547-81.

9. *Congressional Record,* daily ed., July 31, 1973, S 15164-91.

10. U. S. House of Representatives, Committee on Education and Labor, *Comprehensive Manpower Act of 1973.* Report No. 93-659. 93rd Congress, 1st Session, 1973.

11. *Congressional Record,* daily ed., Nov. 28, 1973, H 10220-86.

12. *Congressional Record,* daily ed., Dec. 5, 1973, S 21924-43.

13. U. S. House of Representatives, *Comprehensive Employment and Training Act of 1973,* Report No. 93-737, 93rd Congress, 1st Session, 1973.

14. *Congressional Record,* daily ed., Dec. 20, 1973, H 11793-807 and S 23613-26.

15. *Federal Register,* vol. 39, no. 54 (Mar. 19, 1974), pp. 10,374 –10,403.

16. *Manpower Information Service,* Bureau of National Affairs, vol. 5, no. 10 (Jan. 30, 1974), p. 175.

17. S 2933, 93rd Congress.

18. U. S. Congress, Joint Economic Committee, *The 1974 Economic Report of President,* 93rd Congress, 2nd Session, 1974, vol. I. p. 80.

19. See chap. 14, n. 7.

20. *The Budget of the United States Government, Fiscal Year 1975* (Washington: U. S. Government Printing Office, 1975), p. 115.

21. U. S. House of Representatives, *Second Supplemental Appro-*

priations Bill, 1974, House Report 93-977, 93rd Congress, 2nd Session, 1974.

22. *Congressional Record,* daily ed., Apr. 10, 1974, H 2821-2831.

23. *U. S. Senate, Second Supplemental Appropriations Bill, 1974,* Senate Report 93-814, 93rd Congress, 2nd Session, 1974.

24. *Congressional Record,* daily ed., May 7, 1974, S 7285-86.

25. U. S. House of Representatives, *Making Supplemental Appropriations,* House Report 93-1070, 93rd Congress, 2nd Session, 1974.

26. *Congressional Record,* daily ed., June 4, 1974, H 4706; and June 5, 1974, H 59660.

27. P.L. 93-305.

28. U. S. House of Representatives, *Department of Labor and Health, Education and Welfare, and Related Agencies Appropriation Bill, 1975,* House Report 93-1140, 93rd Congress, 2nd Session, 1974.

29. *Congressional Record,* daily ed. June 27, 1974, H 5943-51.

30. U. S. Senate, *Departments of Labor, and Health, Education and Welfare, and Related Agencies Appropriation Bill, 1975,* Senate Report 93-1146, 93rd Congress, 2nd Session.

31. *Congressional Record,* daily ed., Sept. 16, 1974, S 16674-88.

32. *Manpower Information Service,* vol. 6, no. 4 (Nov. 6, 1974), p. 76.

33. U. S. House of Representatives, *Making Appropriations for the Departments of Labor and Health, Education and Welfare and Related Agencies* House Report 93-1489, 93rd Congress, 2nd Session.

34. *Congressional Record,* daily ed., Nov. 26, 1974, H 11098, S 20251.

35. P. L. 93-517.

36. Congressional Record, daily ed., Oct. 8, 1974, H 10120-23.

37. H. R. 17218, 93rd Congress.

38. S. 4129, 93rd Congress

39. U. S. Congress, Joint Economic Committee, *An Action Program to Reduce Inflation and Restore Economic Growth,* Committee Print, Sept. 21, 1974, 93rd Congress, 2nd Session.

40. H. R. 16596, H. R. 16926, H. R. 16607, H. R. 16150, 93rd Congress.

41. S. 2933 and S. 4079, 93rd Congress.

42. H. R. 15476, 93rd Congress.

43. S. 3947, 93rd Congress.

44. U. S. House of Representatives, Committee on Education and Labor, Select Commitee on Labor, *The Emergency Jobs Act of 1974,* 93rd Congress, Second Session, 1974.

45. U. S. House of Representatives, *Emergency Jobs Act of 1974,* House Report 93-1528, 93rd Congress, 2nd Session, 1974.

46. *Congressional Record,* daily ed., Dec. 12, 1974, H 11698-726.

47. U. S. Senate, Committee on Labor and Welfare, Subcommittee on Employment, Poverty, and Migratory Labor, *Public Service Employment Legislation, 1974,* 93rd Congress, 2nd Session, 1974.

48. U. S. Senate, *Special Employment Assistance Act of 1974,* Senate Report 93-1327, 93rd Congress, 2nd Session, 1974.

49. *Congressional Record,* daily ed., Dec. 12, 1974, S 21031.

50. U. S. House of Representatives, *Public Service Employment,* House Report 93-1621, 93rd Congress, Second Session, 1974.

51. *Congressional Record,* daily ed., Dec. 18, 1974, H 12236, S 21988.

52. P. L. 93-567.

53. U. S. House of Representatives, *Urgent Supplemental Appropriations,* House Report 93-1616; U. S. Senate, *Urgent Supplemental Appropriations, 1975,* Senate Report 93-1406; U. S. House of Representatives, *Making Urgent Supplemental Appropriations,* House Report 93-1641; and *Congressional Record,* daily ed., Dec. 18, 1974, H 12249; Dec. 9, 1974, S 22116; H 12506; S 22272.

54. P. L. 93-624.

55. *Federal Register,* vol. 40, no. 7 (Jan. 10, 1975), pp. 2,360 –2,369.

56. *Manpower Information Service,* vol. 6, no. 10 (Jan. 29, 1975), p. 214–15.

57. H. R. 2584, H. R. 1609, H. R. 4295, S. 472, S. 609, S. 1695, 94th Congress.

58. U. S. House of Representatives, *Emergency Employment Appropriations Act, 1975,* House Report 94-52, 94th Congress, 1st Session.

59. *Congressional Record,* daily ed., Mar. 12, 1975, pp. H 1,566 –1,602.

60. U. S. Senate, *The Emergency Employment Appropriation Act, 1975,* Senate Report 94-91, 94th Congress, 1st Session.

61. *Congressional Record,* daily ed., Apr. 25, 1975, pp. S 6,820–50.

62. U. S. House of Representatives, *Emergency Employment Appropriations for the Fiscal Year Ending June 30, 1975,* House Report 94-201, 94th Congress, 1st Session.

63. *Congressional Record,* daily ed., May 14, 1975, pp. H 4,044 –55; May 15, 1975, pp. S 8553-59.

64. *Congressional Record,* daily ed., June 4, 1975, pp. H 4,858–74.

65. *Congressional Record,* daily ed., June 10, 1975, pp. H 5206–11; June 12, 1975, S 10,527–33, 75–77.

66. P. L. 94-36.

67. H. J. Res. 499.

68. P. L. 94-41.

69. H. R. 1609.

70. H. R. 2584.

71. H. R. 4295.

72. S. 472 and S. 609.

73. S. 1695.

INDEX